THE TEA COUNCIL'S
guide to the
BEST TEA PLACES

GW00493663

1998

Published by
The Tea Council Ltd
Sir John Lyon House
5 High Timber Street
London
EC4V 3NJ

Compiled by: Jane Pettigrew,
Anita Crocker

Every effort has been made to ensure the accuracy of
this publication. However, the publishers do not hold
themselves responsible for inaccuracies or omissions. The
contents are believed to be correct at the time of going to
press, but changes may have occurred since that time.

ISBN 0 9524872 3 3

Design and origination by Roger Simmons Design
Consultancy Limited, The Studio, Entry Hill, Bath BA2 5LY
Printed by Harlequin Colourprint Ltd, Bristol BS4 5QW

CONTENTS

A member of The Tea Council

The Tea Council

Guild of Tea Shops

Foreword

'Tea is the treasure of the world' writes William Ukers in his book 'All About Tea'. He continues that tea 'proved peculiarly suited to the English scene, and even America may never know afternoon tea as England knows it. Like Henley, it is unique.'

Within the pages of this guide, The Tea Council has provided some background to tea and tea drinking in Britain – where our tea comes from, how it is grown and made, what makes one tea different from another, how tea can enhance the enjoyment and flavour of a meal and how tea is an integral part of healthy lifestyles.

No matter what time of day or occasion, a good cup of tea is always welcome. We can be out shopping, driving, walking, playing tennis, cricket or even boating – that tea shop, tearoom or hotel lounge is a most welcome sight.

Each outlet in The Guild – be it in a city or town centre, village or hamlet, coastal or inland – has been inspected by our panel of professional tea tasters and assessed as meeting The Tea Council standard of excellence. Every member is visited and assessed annually. The Guild members receive a splendid membership pack each year including a plaque and certificate. The plaque – in midnight blue this year – enables you to recognise a tea shop, tearoom or tea lounge which is a current member. You may be assured that it is a place where you can expect to relax and enjoy afternoon tea as it should be served.

Enjoy your tea.

Illtyd Lewis
Executive Director, The Tea Council Ltd

THE GUILD OF TEA SHOPS AND ITS RATIONALE

Tea, our national drink, is served in thousands of outlets across Britain on a daily basis. An independent study commissioned by The Tea Council revealed that very few of these outlets were serving tea to the high standards that The Tea Council believes desirable.

Therefore The Tea Council concluded that recognition should be given only to those establishments which fulfil exacting criteria and meet high standards in serving, selling and preparing tea. This recognition is given by invitation to membership of the unique and prestigious organisation – The Tea Council Guild of Tea Shops.

Membership is limited to one hundred outlets. All establishments must first pass an exacting and incognito inspection by acknowledged tea tasters. Once a shop has become a member, The Tea Council maintains a watching brief on Guild members throughout the year to ensure standards of excellence.

If you know of a tea shop which you think should be a member of The Guild, please write in with the name, address and reason you liked it, and we will be sure to investigate.

Each tea place featured in this guide offers you a pleasant, relaxing and reviving experience at a price which gives good value for money. The Guild of Tea Shops endorses high standards of tea making and serving, home baking, cleanliness and hygiene, staff efficiency and attitude.

Some of the Guild member shops operate a no smoking policy which is represented by the symbol ⊗. This is displayed under the opening times of the tea shops. In next year's guide, we are introducing a symbol denoting wheel chair access.

COME RAIN OR SHINE: TEA IS BRITAIN'S FIRST CHOICE

The British have been drinking tea for more than three hundred years. Today, tea accounts for 42% of everything we drink and 76% of the population drink tea daily. We import about 16% of the producer countries' exports and Britain is a major buyer in the world tea market. In fact, we import more tea than the whole of Europe and North America combined.

A staggering 185 million cups of tea a day are drunk in Britain. By the time British tea drinkers reach the ripe old age of 'three score years and ten', we shall each have drunk an estimated 90,000 cups of tea. So we drink 8.39 units of fluid per person per day (a unit being 7 fluid ounces). Statistically tea accounts for 3.38 units, coffee 1.69 units, alcohol 1.41 units, soft drinks 1.6 units and others 0.31 units a day.

Tea has influenced our history, culture and society. The growth of the British potteries and the ship building industry are indebted to tea. In the second half of the eighteenth century, British potteries such as Spode, Worcester, Derby and Wedgwood were producing tea wares. In 1850, the first British clipper, *The Stornaway*, was built in Aberdeen. These new, faster ships cut the journey time radically from China to British shores. The *Cutty Sark* is our most famous clipper. Many of our famous authors and poets have written hundreds of lines describing the nation's favourite drink: Samuel Pepys, Dr Johnson, Lewis Carroll, Noel Coward to name just a few. Our nation's leaders have always relied on the virtues of tea. Wellington, while fighting at Waterloo, was said to stop for a quick cup while encouraging his troops to victory. Gladstone is reputed to have filled his hot water bottle with tea enabling him both to warm his feet and quench his thirst throughout the night.

A POTTED HISTORY OF TEA

Tea is indigenous to both China and India and both countries tell their own legends about the discovery of tea. China's Shen Nung, often described as an emperor, was resting under a tree in 2737 BC. Whilst boiling some water, a leaf from a nearby wild tea tree fell into the pot. He drank the brew and liked it. By the time of the Tang Dynasty (906–618 BC), tea was China's national drink. The modern word 'tea' derives from the early Chinese words *cha* and *te* used to describe both the beverage and leaf.

Buddhist monks are reputed to have spread the tea drinking habit around the East by cultivating tea gardens in the grounds of monasteries and royal palaces. In about 552 AD, the monks took tea to Japan where they not only cultivated the tea drinking habit but also pioneered tea cultivation in that country.

According to the American author, William Ukers, a Persian merchant – Hajji Mahommed – brought the first knowledge of tea to Europe. Mahommed described his travels of Cathay to the Venetian author Giambattista Ramusio. He claimed people 'made use of another plant or rather its leaves. This is called Chai Chatai and grows in the district of Cathay which is called Caican-fu (Szechwan).' In 1559, Ramusio published Volume II of his 'Voyages and Travels' in which he described how tea was made and drunk by the people of Cathay.

The Portuguese and the Dutch may be credited with the spread of tea drinking and trading in Europe in the late sixteenth and early seventeenth centuries. The Portuguese pioneered the shipping routes to the East. The famous Vasco da Gama sailed around the Cape of Good Hope in 1497 and sailed on to Malacca on the Malay Peninsula. In 1516 he reached China. The Dutch navigator and writer, Jan Hugo van Linschooten, persuaded Dutch captains and traders that it would be more profitable to open up their own direct trading routes. From 1595, they did this and regular shipments of tea were brought back to the ports of France, Holland and Portugal.

At this time the British East India Company had opened up the trading routes to the East but concentrated on spices and silks. Since the first British ships did not reach China until 1637, tea until then was probably purchased from Dutch traders. In 1637 the British set up trading contacts with Chinese merchants and in 1644 established themselves in the port of Amoy. This was their principal base in China for almost a century.

The first mention of tea by an Englishman is dated 27th June 1615; an East Indian agent in Japan wrote to another in China requesting 'a pot of chaw'. The first British sale of tea was in 1657, when Thomas Garaway, tobacconist and coffee shop keeper, served and sold tea in his shop in Exchange Alley in the City of London. In 1660 he published a broadsheet extolling the virtues of the beverage and its health benefits. In 1658 the London newspaper, Mercurius Politicus, published the first advertisement for the sale of tea at the Sultaness Head Coffee House, Sweetings Rents by the Royal Exchange in London. So the fashion of

drinking tea began in the coffee houses of London – the forerunners of gentlemen's clubs. The Portuguese princess Catherine of Braganza, the wife of Charles II, introduced tea to the royal palace and court in 1662. Tea gradually became a fashionable drink first for the rich and famous and later for the general population.

In the seventeenth century tea was expensive since it was not only a rare commodity but also heavily taxed. The East India Company had their charter, granted by Elizabeth I, revised twice. In 1669 it was given the British trading monopoly in the East and imports from Holland were banned. The Tea Act of 1773 further revised the charter giving the company monopoly of British trading with China and India plus import rights in the colonies. So colonials were asked to pay the same duties on imports, particularly of tea, as the British. This resulted in the Boston Tea Party and culminated in the War of Independence. The high cost of tea led to smuggling, adulteration of leaves and a thriving black market. These practices continued until 1784 when William Pitt the

Younger had the Commutation law passed by Parliament which reduced tax from 112% to 12.5%. In 1834 Parliament passed another act revoking the East India's monopoly on trading which opened the way for free trade.

At the turn of the nineteenth century Anna, seventh Duchess of Bedford, started taking tea in the afternoon to stave off hunger pangs between lunch and supper which left her with a 'sinking feeling'. So, afternoon tea became fashionable. In the 1830s, the temperance reformers saw tea as the ideal means of combating British alcoholic beverage consumption. They held tea meetings in Liverpool, Birmingham and Preston which were often attended by over two thousand people. Tea was served at these meetings which inspired the creation of the tearoom. Then in 1864 the manageress of the London Bridge branch of The Aerated Bread Company asked her directors if she could serve and sell tea to customers when they came in for their bread. They agreed and hence the tea shop was born.

Brewing a Good Cup of Tea

- Use a good quality loose leaf or bagged tea
- Always use freshly drawn boiling water
- Measure the tea carefully: use one tea bag or one rounded teaspoon of loose tea for each cup to be served
- Allow the tea to brew for the recommended time before pouring

TEA	COUNTRY OF ORIGIN	BREWING TIME	MILK/BLACK/ LEMON*	CHARACTERISTICS
DARJEELING	INDIA	3–5 minutes	BLACK or MILK	Delicate, slightly astringent flavour
ASSAM	INDIA	3–5 minutes	BLACK or MILK	Full-bodied with a rich, smooth, malty flavour
CEYLON BLEND	SRI LANKA	3–5 minutes	BLACK or MILK	Brisk, full flavour with a bright colour
KENYA	KENYA	2–4 minutes	BLACK or MILK	A strong tea with a brisk flavour
EARL GREY	CHINA OR INDIA	3–5 minutes	BLACK or LEMON	Flavoured with the natural oil of citrus bergamot fruit
LAPSANG SOUCHONG	CHINA	3–5 minutes	BLACK	Smoky aroma and flavour
CHINA OOLONG	CHINA	5–7 minutes	BLACK	Subtle, delicate, lightly flavoured tea

*The addition of lemon is a matter of personal preference.

A PROFILE OF TEA

Tea is an evergreen plant of the camellia family and is known as camellia sinensis. Tea varies in characteristics and flavour according to the type of soil, the altitude and the climatic conditions of the area in which it grows. Other factors are the method by which it is processed and blended.

PRODUCTION TECHNIQUES

When people talk of making tea, they are talking about the manufacturing and processing of the plucked leaves. There are three types of tea 'make' – black, oolong and green.

BLACK TEA holds the largest percentage of the worldwide tea market and there are five stages in its manufacture:

1. *Withering:* the plucked leaf is spread out on trays and left to wither.

2. *Rolling or Cut Tear and Curl:* the withered leaf is broken so that the natural juices and enzymes are released. Orthodox production uses the original type of machine that rolls the leaves to break the veins. CTC or Unorthodox production uses more modern machines to Cut Tear and Curl the leaves.

3. *Fermentation:* the broken leaf is spread on trays or laid out in troughs. On contact with the air, oxidation or fermentation takes place. The leaves are left for 3–4 hours.

4. *Drying:* the oxidised leaf is fed through a warm chamber where remaining moisture is extracted.

5. *Sorting:* the black tea is graded by a series of sieves into leaf sizes.

OOLONG TEA undergoes the same process as black tea but the fermentation time is halved.

GREEN TEA: The plucked leaf is allowed to wither. It is then steamed and dried. The result is small grey-green pieces of tea.

LEAF GRADES

Grade is the term used by the tea trade to describe the size of leaf particle. The term has nothing to do with leaf quality. There are two main categories – leaf and broken leaf – known in the trade as Pekoe and Broken Pekoe. 'Pekoe' is derived from the Chinese word which describes the 'down' on the back of a white tea leaf. A Pekoe grade is virtually a whole leaf. Broken Pekoe is the largest leaf particles. Fannings are smaller particles and divide into three or four numerical classifications of decreasing size: Fl, F2, F3 and F4. Dust is the trade term used to describe the smallest leaf particle.

SPECIALITY TEAS

Speciality teas are teas that take their name from the area or country in which they are grown; a blend of teas for a particular time of day; a blend of teas named after a person; or a blend of teas to which fruit oils, flower petals or blossoms have been added, thus scenting the tea.

CHINA
Gunpowder

A green tea which, after it has been withered, is steamed and rolled into small pellets without breaking the veins in the tea leaves. These are then dried, and when brewed with boiling water, produce a very light, refreshing and pale-coloured tea. The name is said to have been given to the tea because the pellets look like gunshot or gunpowder of years gone by.

Jasmine

China tea which has been dried with jasmine blossoms placed between the layers of tea. The tea therefore has a light, delicate aroma of jasmine and a flavour to match.

Keemun

A black China tea, bright in colour with a round nutty flavour.

Lapsang Souchong

A large leaf tea distinguished by its smoky aroma and flavour. The story goes that when the Chinese first discovered tea, they used to dry it in the sun. Chinese legend claims that the smoking process was discovered by accident. At some point in China's history, an army camped in a tea factory that was full of drying leaves awaiting processing and so held up the normal working routine. When the soldiers left, the workers needed to prepare the leaves for the market as quickly as possible, so they lit open fires of pine wood to speed up the drying. The tea reached the market on time and a new flavour had been created. Today, the tea is still smoked but by more hygienic, modern methods.

INDIA
Assam

A blend of tea grown in Assam in North India. It is a full-bodied tea with a dark liquor and a rich malty flavour which is ideal as the first cup of tea in the morning. It really wakes you up. Such teas

14

are used in everyday popular blends because of the full-bodied richness.

Darjeeling

Known as the 'Champagne of Teas', Darjeeling is grown several thousands of feet above sea level in the foothills of the Himalayan mountains. Darjeeling teas have a very light delicate flavour.

Nilgiri

The tea from the Nilgiri Hills in Southern India is light, bright and delicate in taste.

SRI LANKA (CEYLON)
Ceylon Blend

Ceylon teas span the entire spectrum of tea production, from low to high grown teas. By blending teas from different areas of the island, Sri Lanka is able to offer a very wide choice of flavour and characteristics. Some blends are full-bodied, others are light and delicate, but all are brisk, full-flavoured and have a bright colour.

Dimbula

Grown 5,000 ft above sea level in Sri Lanka, Dimbula teas are light and bright in colour with a crisp, strong flavour

which leaves the mouth feeling fresh and clean. Dimbula was one of the first areas of Sri Lanka to be planted with tea after the demise of the coffee estates in 1870.

Uva

A fine flavoured tea from the eastern slopes of the Central Mountains of Sri Lanka. Uva tea is bright in colour, has a dry crisp taste and makes an ideal mid-morning or after lunch tea.

KENYA

Tea from Kenya is very bright and colourful, which makes it easily distinguishable from its Asian counterparts. It has a reddish, coppery tint with a pleasant, brisk flavour. Kenya tea is widely used in tea bag blends and is an ideal drink at any time of the day or night.

INDONESIA

Indonesian teas are light and flavoursome. Most are sold for blending purposes as this produces good financial rewards in terms of foreign currency for the country. However, in recent years, it has become possible to buy Indonesian tea as a speciality tea. It is extremely refreshing taken without milk, garnished with a slice of lemon, making it an ideal drink for the figure conscious.

SPECIALITY TEA BLENDS
English Breakfast

Traditionally a blend of Assam and Ceylon teas that gives pungency and flavour to help digest a full English breakfast and give a good brisk start to the day. Today, many English Breakfast blends also include an East African tea from Malawi, Tanzania, Zimbabwe or Kenya which gives the blend a coppery brightness.

Afternoon Tea

Traditionally, a blend of delicate Darjeeling tea and high-grown Ceylon tea to produce a refreshing but light tea which makes an ideal companion to cucumber sandwiches, cream pastries and fruit cakes.

Earl Grey

Traditionally, a blend of black China teas treated with the natural oils of the citrus bergamot fruit which gives the blend its perfumed aroma and flavour. Earl Grey tea is said to have originally been blended for the second Earl Grey by a mandarin after Britain had completed a successful diplomatic mission to China.

House Blend

Some menus offer 'a pot of tea', others 'a pot of house blend tea'. This tea is equivalent to – if not better than – the type of tea the majority of us buy to use at home. In tea trade language, it is known as a 'popular brand leading blend'. In catering terms, it will be a Quality Award tea, as identified by The Tea Council's Catering Tea Quality Programme. No matter whether it is loose leaf or in a tea bag, a house blend tea is a work of art. It can contain 15–35 different teas which are blended in order to achieve the consistent quality, flavour and characteristics consumers expect from their favourite 'popular brand leading blend'. Some of the teas are seasonal, some are not. During the year or plucking season, adverse weather conditions can affect the quality of any of the teas, in which case the blender has to find other teas that will produce the same flavour and characteristics and ensure the consistency and quality of the blend. To do this, a taster/blender will taste between 200 and 1,000 teas a day and will adjust the 'recipe' so that we can enjoy our favourite cup of tea all day, and everyday.

FLAVOURED TEAS

Flavoured teas are real tea (*Camellia sinensis*) blended with fruit, spices or herbs. For example, fruit flavoured teas such as apple, lemon, orange, mango or blackcurrant consist of tea blended with pieces of fruit peel or blossom or treated with the natural fruit juice or oil (known as the zest). Spiced tea, such as cinnamon or nutmeg, is tea blended with a particular spice, and herb flavoured teas have the dried herb added to the blend, as in the case of mint or sage tea.

In all cases, the fruit, spice or herb flavours the real tea and should not be confused with herbal or fruit infusions, which contain no tea.

TISANES AND FRUIT INFUSIONS

Tisane, according to Roget's Thesaurus, is a soft drink or a tonic. Stemming from the French, the term is used to describe infusions of mainly herbal leaves such as camomile, peppermint, nettle, etc and does not contain real tea. Fruit infusions – today known as fruit teas – like herbal infusions, do not contain one leaf of real tea. The zest, dried pieces of peel or fruit blossoms, are blended with dried hibiscus leaves to produce a refreshing fruit flavoured infusion.

HOW TO CHOOSE A GOOD TEA AND STORE IT

When a tea taster, whether a producer, buyer or seller, looks at a tea, there are certain things that he or she can tell by just looking.

For example, the tea must appear 'even'. This means that the dry leaf sample the taster examines is all of the same leaf particle size. Not only does it give the dry leaf a pleasing appearance, but it does mean that when brewed, the flavour and pungency are all released from the leaf simultaneously. An uneven blend – leaf of varying particle sizes – means that when brewing, the flavour and pungency are released according to the varying sizes of leaf particle, giving an unbalanced overall flavour and quality.

Keep your tea in an airtight caddy in a cool dry storage area, away from other strong smelling foods as tea absorbs other flavours very easily.

THE ART OF
TEA TASTING

Tea tasters train for five years and most of them will tell you that they go on learning the art for the rest of their lives. Tea brokers and buyers taste samples of the tea which are to be sold at auction and price them accordingly. Tasters check the colour of the dry leaf, smell the wet leaf and tea liquor, then sip and slurp the liquor itself. In all cases, they are looking for quality and flavour. They also make comparisons with tea from the same estates. Tasters working with specific companies are also looking for the qualities and flavours which will keep your favourite blend consistent day in day out, year after year.

Experiment with different teas to find your favourite, or you might like to blend your own. A few leaves of Lapsang Souchong or Earl Grey added to your everyday tea will give it a completely new flavour.

Tea tasters use a wide vocabulary to describe the appearance and flavour of tea. The following are the terms used most frequently for the taste of the tea liquor:

Baggy: an unpleasant taste, resulting from tea being carried or wrapped in unlined hessian bags.

Bakey: an over-fired tea which means too much moisture has been taken from the leaf while drying.

Bitter: an unpleasant taste associated with raw teas.

Body: a liquor having both fullness and strength.

Bright: denotes a lively fresh tea with good keeping quality.

Brisk: the most 'live' characteristic, results from good manufacture.

Coloury: indicates useful depth of colour and strength.

Earthy: caused by damp storage of tea but can also describe a taste that is sometimes 'climatically inherent' in teas from certain regions.

Empty: a liquor lacking fullness; with no substance.

Fruity: can be due to over-fermenting during manufacture and/or bacterial infection before firing or drying. Unlike wine, this is not a desirable taste.

Hard: a very pungent liquor; a desirable quality in tea.

Malty: a desirable character in some Assam teas. A full, bright tea with a malty taste.

Mature: not bitter or flat.

Muscatel: a desirable character in Darjeeling teas.

Musty: a hint of mould.

Plain: a liquor that is clean but lacking in desirable characteristics.

Point: a bright, acidic and penetrating characteristic.

Rasping: a very course and harsh liquor.

Thick: liquor with good colour and strength.

Weedy: a grass/hay taste associated with teas that have been under withered during manufacture.

If you would like to learn more tea vocabulary, please look up the Glossary on our website: http://www.teacouncil.co.uk.

TEA PAIRINGS

Despite being our national drink, there is just one time in the day when tea gives way to a competitive drink, coffee, after dinner. Coffee is usually taken in preference to tea despite the fact that tea, unlike coffee, is a digestif which calms and soothes a full stomach and cleans the palate – of key importance when a final glass of wine or liqueur is being enjoyed after the meal.

In addition, teas can be paired with specific foods and wines in order to enhance both the food and the wine whilst highlighting the specific qualities of the teas themselves.

Working with The Academy of Food and Wine, The Tea Council has identi-fied specific pairings to demonstrate these exciting possibilities. Pairings can be created to partner special desserts, cheeses, foods and liqueurs. Pairings may also be a feature of afternoon tea.

The Tea Council commissioned research which revealed that 53% of the restaurants in the UK fail to offer tea on their menus and only 22% of customers request tea when it is not featured. This suggests that the hotel and restaurant trade is losing revenue of £260 million by not offering tea.

The matrix illustrates tea's potential as an ideal after-dinner or after-lunch digestif, as well as giving ample choice for a delicious afternoon tea.

TEA	SANDWICHES	AFTERNOON TEA PASTRIES/DESSERTS	CHEESE	WINE	LIQUEUR
Ceylon	Cucumber or Tomato Sandwich	Tarte Au Citron	Mature Cheddar	Fine dessert wine	Chartreuse yellow/green
Kenya	Beef and Horseradish or Ham Sandwich	Chocolate Cake (rich)	Austrian Smoked	New World Cabernet Sauvignon	Drambuie
Darjeeling	Cream Cheese or Egg and Cress Sandwich	Cream Desserts	Cream Cheese	Zinfandel type wines Shiraz or Syrah	Armagnac
Lapsang	Chicken or Smoked Salmon Sandwich	Walnut Cake	Stilton	New World Chardonnay	Tawny Port
Earl Grey	Fine Pâté or Ham and Mustard Sandwich	Crème Brûlée	Leicester	Valpolicella or Beaujolais	

TEA AND HEALTH

Tea is a natural product. It contains no artificial colouring, preservatives or flavouring and is virtually calorie free if taken without milk or sugar.

Tea provides an extremely pleasant way of taking in the right amount of fluid that our bodies need daily for optimum health. Tea also contains trace elements and vitamins which help to supplement the body's needs if it is drunk in conjunction with a healthy diet.

Tea is a rich source of two minerals that are essential to health – manganese and potassium. Manganese is needed for bone growth and the body's development. Five or six cups of tea a day will provide 45% of the body's daily requirement. Potassium is vital for maintaining a normal heartbeat and, as one of the major constituents in living cells, it helps to balance sodium, enables nerves and muscles to function and regulates fluid levels within the cells. The same five or six cups of tea drunk daily will provide 25% of the body's needs.

Tea also contains small amounts of the following vitamins: carotene, a precursor to vitamin A, which has antioxidant properties; thiamin (vitamin B1) and riboflavin (vitamin B2) – both essential for releasing energy from food; nicotinic acid and pantothenic acid, which are nutrients linked to the water-soluble vitamins, and ascorbic acid (vitamin C), essential for a healthy immune system.

Tea also contains caffeine. An average cup of tea made from loose leaf or tea bag tea contains 40 milligrams of caffeine, and made from instant tea, 30 milligrams. Caffeine is a mild stimulant which can increase concentration and alertness, accuracy and sensitivity of taste and smell. In high doses (more than 800 milligrams, or some 20 cups of tea a day) it can invoke anxiety and unpleasant gastric sensations.

Tea helps us digest our foods and acts as a diuretic. Tea cools, calms, refreshes and relaxes. For more information, http:\\www.teahealth.co.uk

THE TEA CLUB

The Tea Club exists so that its members can share and enjoy the history, traditions and romance associated with this fascinating drink.

When you join you will receive a letter of welcome, a membership card, a complimentary sample of tea, a copy of the current Tea Club magazine and a Tea Club mug.

Membership costs £12 UK, £18 Europe and £25 Worldwide.

THE MAGAZINE & NEWSLETTER

This sixteen page magazine is mailed to you three times a year. It is packed full of information tea lovers will adore. It is a bright and absorbing publication featuring detailed articles about tea. It includes the latest reviews of books relating to tea. Collectors' Corner in the magazine provides you with tea associated articles at discounted prices. You are also entitled to a 10% discount on any Tea Council mail order offer. And you receive a Tea Club newsletter three times a year giving the latest news about events, special offers and fun competitions.

EVENTS

Each year, special events are organised. Previously tea parties have been held at the Café Royal, Claridges and The Waldorf. In 1997, The Tea Club made a trip to Sandringham. Members were privileged to visit the Royal Stud Farm, before Congham Hall for afternoon tea.

For more information, please contact:

The Membership Secretary
The Tea Club
PO Box 221, Guildford
SURREY GU1 3YT

THE TEA COUNCIL

The Tea Council is an independent, non-profit making organisation funded by the UK tea trade and the governments of seven tea producing countries. Its aim is to promote tea generically in the United Kingdom.

Its main activities are:

■ The promotion of tea as a natural and healthy beverage.

■ Researching the role of tea in a healthy lifestyle.

■ Internet website –The Tea Council has two developing sites: the main site and a second site dedicated to tea and health.

■ Education resources for primary, secondary and further education.

■ The Catering Tea Quality Programme which monitors the quality of catering tea and assures its quality standards, whilst providing a database through which caterers can check the quality of the tea they are using.

■ The creation and administration of The Guild of Tea Shops.

■ The Tea Club.

■ The Tea Council runs various awards throughout the year to highlight and promote the importance of making, serving and selling good quality tea: **Top Tea Place of the Year, The Best Motorways Cup of Tea** and **The Best Inflight Cup of Tea**.

■ Tea Pairings.

For more information, please write to:
The Tea Council Limited
Sir John Lyon House
5 High Timber Street
London EC4V 3NJ
Tel: 0171 248 1024
Fax: 0171 329 4568
http:\\www.teacouncil.co.uk
email: tea@teacouncil.co.uk

A member of The Tea Council

The Tea Council

Guild of Tea Shops

S O U T H   W E S T
R E G I O N A L   M A P

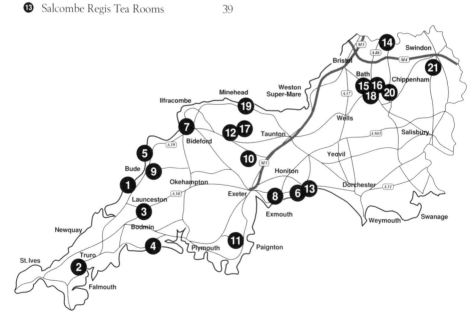

CARPENTER'S KITCHEN

Owners: Debbie and Geoff Beszant

The Harbour, Boscastle
Cornwall PL35 0ND
Tel: 01840 250595

Directions
Take the B3266 from Camelford or the B3263 from Tintagel. Follow signs to Boscastle Harbour.

Opening times
Open April–October, daily 10.30–5.30 pm.
March and November, weekends only,
10.30 am–5 pm. Christmas, 27th December–
1st January inclusive 10.30 am–5 pm.
Now available, small amount of seating outside.

Awards
1996 Tea Council Award of Excellence

Local Interest:
Walk around this fascinating typically Cornish village with its narrow lanes and old cottages. Also explore the site of Bottreaux Castle and 60 acres of the surrounding National Trust cliffs and land with walks in all directions and fantastic views.

The site of Carpenter's Kitchen was used as a carpenter's workshop for almost one hundred years. When the last owner, Arthur Olde, retired in 1987, his daughter, Debbie, and son-in-law, Geoff, recognised the potential of the site, hence the now thriving tearoom. From the front door there is a view over the river and harbour, and a small amount of seating is available on the forecourt. Inside, Geoff and Debbie have kept the rustic country style with polished wooden furniture, a traditional dado rail, wooden floor and wisteria stencilled walls that are hung with old photographs and paintings of old Boscastle and carpenters who previously worked here.

The menu is designed to incorporate all the home cooking that makes Carpenter's Kitchen so popular with local people and visitors. There is a daily selection of goodies in the cold cabinet, and the sweet trolley usually holds some real favourites such as meringues, cheesecake and fruit pies. And if you can't be tempted by the cakes, clotted cream can be dolloped on freshly baked scones or Cornish splits. Seasonal treats include fresh Port Isaac crab in the summer, and freshly prepared soups for chilly spring and autumn days. *Teas served:* House Blend (a blend of Indian and Kenya teas), Earl Grey, Darjeeling, Assam, Lapsang Souchong, Lemon. *Fruit flavoured teas and herbal infusions are also available.*

CHARLOTTE'S TEA-HOUSE

Owners: Tony and Cynthia Martin

**Coinage Hall
No 1 Boscawen Street
Truro, Cornwall TR1 2QU
Tel: 01872 261133**

Directions
The Coinage Hall is in the centre of Truro, opposite the Hall for Cornwall, directly behind the bronze War Memorial. Charlotte's is on the top floor.

Opening times
Open all year.
Monday–Saturday, 10 am–5 pm.
Sunday, closed.

Local Interest:
Truro is the administrative centre of the Duchy of Cornwall, home to the County Museum, and central to all the county's resorts and places of historical interest. The fine 19th century cathedral dominates the excellent shopping centre.

The Coinage Hall in Truro has a history that goes back to 1302 and the halcyon days of Cornish tin mining, but the present Grade II listed building was built in 1848 and has recently been lovingly restored by Tony and Cynthia. Charlotte's Tea-House, on the top floor of the building, is the realisation of their dream of creating a sanctuary of Victorian tranquillity just a few steps from the city's busy streets. The ambience is enhanced by crystal chandeliers and period furniture, home-made cakes served on silver-plated cake stands, and waitresses in period costume.

The emphasis is on quality, and every care is taken to provide the best. Everything on the menu is made on the premises and there is always a tempting display of cakes. Light lunches include potato toasties, omelettes and salads, and there are cream teas and Charlotte's speciality high teas – all made to order. Visitors can browse in the antique showrooms, or visit the wonderful selection of Italian drapes on the same floor as the tearoom, or on Mondays and Tuesdays, the ground floor displays of household and Victorian furniture. Local crafts are on show on Wednesday and Thursday, and quality collectibles and antiques on Friday and Saturday. *Teas served:* House Blend, Assam, Ceylon, China Yunnan, Darjeeling, Earl Grey, Lady Grey, Jasmine, Lapsang Souchong. *Fruit flavoured teas and herbal infusions are also available.*

MAD HATTER'S

Owner: Vicki James

28 Church Street
Launceston, Cornwall
PL15 8AR
Tel: 01566 777188

Directions

Launceston is just off the A30 in North Cornwall.
Mad Hatter's is in the centre of the town, 30 yards
from the town square, opposite WH Smiths.

Opening times
Open summer, 9.30 am–7 pm except
Sunday, 11 am–5 pm and Wednesday,
9.30 am–5.30 pm.
Winter, 10 am–5.30 pm every day
except Sunday. Opening times vary:
please telephone to confirm.

Local Interest:
*Launceston is the ancient capital of Cornwall and there is
a castle run by English Heritage, a museum and a Town
Trail which walks you past all the interesting landmarks
of the town.*

Vicki James doesn't believe that quality and high standards have to be at the expense of entertainment, and admits that being "as Mad as a Hatter" helped in creating this very idiosyncratic tearoom where Lewis Carroll's characters are everywhere. On Saturdays and holidays, she is even to be seen serving tea dressed as her alter ego in top hat and tails. Vicki designed and decorated the shop herself and created the wonderfully humorous menu that offers Mad Hatter's Platters of cheese, tuna or smoked ham with bread and pickles, Alice's Scrumptious Sandwiches, March Hare's Marvellous Cakes and Mad Hatter's Specials. A new range of very popular toasted sandwiches includes a Mouldy Old Dough (stilton and mushroom) and even Call the Paramedics! (raspberry jam, chocolate chips and bananas served with clotted cream). But the favourite item has to be the Indecisive Cake Taster whereby those tempted by several of the home-made, calorie-laden gateaux can sample any three or, in desperation, ask the waitress to choose for them. Also featured – a special Dormouse selection of delicious food lower in saturated fat and sugar and higher in fibre, and foods suitable for diabetics. *Teas served:* Assam, Ceylon, China, Darjeeling, Earl Grey, English Breakfast, Jasmine, Kenya, Lapsang Souchong, Mad Hatter's Special Blend (lightly spiced). *Scented teas and herbal infusions are also available.*

THE PLANTATION CAFE

Owners: Ann and Maurice Vaughan

The Coombes, Polperro
Cornwall PL13 2RG
Tel: 01503 272223

Directions

Park in the main car park and walk to the Plantation Cafe which is on the right hand side of the main road, half way between the car park and the harbour.

Opening times
Open April–end September.
Monday–Friday, 10.30 am–5.30 pm
(9 pm in peak season).
Saturday, closed.
Sunday, 10.30 am–5.30 pm.

Local Interest:
Polperro is a traditional fishing village once well known for its smuggling. Visit the new Teglio Museum that tells the history of Polperro and South East Cornwall and take a pleasure trip in a fishing boat to see the coves and the caves along the coast. Also look out for the stories about Piskeys, the Cornish fairy folk, and their Queen, Joan of Wad, and King Sam Spriggin.

In the vigorous days of Victorian expansion and enterprise, a local Polperro man went off adventuring in North America and made a fortune on the plantations there. He later returned to the place where he was born and used some of the money to build this black and white house right beside the River Pol – hence the name of the tearoom. The building stands in a conservation area so its solid, secure Victorian exterior of traditional Cornish stone and Delabole slate roof will never change. Inside, the Victorian theme is continued with exposed black and white beams, an open fireplace with its copper hood, oak tables, wheelback chairs, copper and brass pots and pans and collections of teapots and Delft ware to decorate the walls.

The river runs peacefully alongside the lovingly-tended garden that has won awards for its beauty and colour and provides a stunning setting for lunch or tea. The menu offers all sorts of local specialities – Cornish pasties, cheese and onion pies, sandwiches made with locally caught crab, and delicious home-made cakes, scones and fruit pies served with Cornish clotted cream. Real traditional Cornish treats! *Teas served:* House Blend, Earl Grey, Assam, Darjeeling, Lapsang Souchong, Ceylon. *Fruit flavoured teas and herbal infusions are also offered.*

RECTORY TEAROOMS

Owner: Jill Savage

Rectory Farm, Morwenstow
Near Bude, Cornwall EX23 9SR
Tel: 01288 331251

Directions
From the A39, from Bideford to Bude, turn off at the sign to Morwenstow. Follow signs to the village and church. The tearoom is next to the church.

Opening times
Open Easter–end October.
Monday–Thursday and Sunday, 11 am–6 pm.
Friday and Saturday, 11 am–6 pm and 7.30 pm–9.30 pm.

Local Interest:
Only ten minutes away is some of the most spectacular scenery in North Cornwall. Next door is the ancient Church of St John the Baptist and famous graveyard with the graves of shipwrecked sailors.

Rectory Farm has a long long history and is mentioned in a document dated 1296 when it belonged to the monks of St John of Bridgwater. The main hall of the house with its heavy oak beams and ancient stone flagged floor is now the restaurant and tearoom and has been run by the same family for some 40 years. It was the current owner, Jill Savage's mother-in-law, who set it up in 1954 when she realised that a lot of people were passing her door on their walks along the coastal footpath that runs right past the front door. She recognised the potential for a busy tearoom and created a warm, traditional interior with Victorian furniture and chintz curtains and today, there is a steady stream of customers right through the summer season. As well as enjoying high quality lunches, teas and dinners, you can buy local jams, chutneys and other produce from the little shop area.

Visitors come from all over the world to see the church of St John the Baptist, made famous by Parson Hawker, an eccentric who introduced Harvest Festival to British churches and wrote the famous Cornish anthem, 'Trelawney'. Rectory Farm, which is next door, gives them a chance to also enjoy a really good traditional English tea. *Teas served:* India, Earl Grey, Lapsang Souchong, Gunpowder, Keemun, Assam, Jasmine. *Herbal infusions are also offered.*

THE CLOCK TOWER TEAROOMS

Owners: Stewart and June Fraser

**Connaught Gardens
Peak Hill Road, Sidmouth
Devon EX10 8RZ
Tel: 01395 512477**

Directions

From the town centre, proceed to the sea front and turn right. Take the road up a slight incline following signs to Manor Road car park. Connaught Gardens is directly opposite the car park and the tearooms are in the clock tower, at the top of Jacobs Ladder.

Opening times

Open all year except Christmas Day.
Monday–Sunday inclusive, 10 am–5 pm.
Longer hours in summer.

Local Interest:
Sidmouth has two beaches that are good for bathing, sailing and fishing, and the town has good shops, and holiday accommodation. The surrounding countryside offers wonderful walks over the cliffs and headlands.

Previously in a state of ruin, The Clock Tower has been lovingly restored by the Frasers and now offers an unusual and charming venue for lunch or tea. It stands on the remains of ancient lime kilns and once served as a boathouse, but today, the castellated building, with its gothic-style windows, has been brought back to life. The old stone walls cascade with plants and flowers and visitors who choose a table outside in the beautiful gardens can relish the amazing views of the sea and the stunning coastline. Inside, there are low beams decorated with amazing wood carvings by a local artist, and the polished wooden floors and warm tones of the wooden furniture create a relaxed, friendly, welcoming atmosphere.

The selection of hot and cold drinks (including Ovaltine and hot chocolate) and the range of sandwiches and toasties, jacket potatoes, pizzas, ploughmans lunches and tea-time traditionals makes this a good place in both the cold of winter or the blazing heat of summer. There are scones with clotted cream and jam, toasted teacakes and a selection of cakes and gateaux for those with a sweet tooth. *Teas served:* House Blend, Assam, Darjeeling, Earl Grey.

THE COMMODORE HOTEL

Owner: Bruce Woolaway

Marine Parade
Instow, North Devon
EX39 4JN
Tel: 01271 860347
Fax: 01271 861233

Directions
From the M5 take Exit 27 for the North Devon Link Road. Take the turning to Instow signposted just before Torridge Bridge. Follow signs for Instow seafront and these will bring you to Marine Parade.

Opening times
Open to non-residents all year, 7.30 am–9.30 pm. Tea is served from 3–6 pm.

Awards
1997 Top Tea Place of The Year

Local Interest:
The historic towns of Bideford and Barnstaple are nearby and Instow is within easy reach of Exmoor and Dartmoor National Parks.

Originally a Georgian gentleman's residence, this waterside hotel sits elegantly overlooking the mouth of the rivers Taw and Torridge in one of North Devon's prettiest locations. The Woolaways, a local Devon family, have owned the hotel since 1969 and they have created a stylish, welcoming environment where views of the palm trees, sweeping lawns that slope gently down to the sandy shore and the constantly changing waterfront scenery make it a perfect place for afternoon tea. In summer months, relax on the terrace and watch the yachts scudding by with billowing sails, and in the chillier winter months, take shelter from the sea breezes in the comfortable lounge.

The hotel's marine setting is echoed in the menu where a good range of seafoods is offered for lunchtime savouries and in open sandwiches. And, since this is the home of clotted cream, don't miss the cream tea, or, for a change, try a clotted cream ice cream or treat yourself to one of the rich desserts or cakes that are served with generous portions of either the clotted or double variety of the delicious indulgence. *Teas served:* Assam, Darjeeling, Lapsang Souchong, Earl Grey, Traditional PG Tips. *Flavoured teas and herbal infusions are also offered.*

THE COSY TEAPOT

Owners: Pat and Norman Palmer

13 Fore Street, Budleigh Salterton
Devon EX9 6NH
Tel: 01395 444016

Directions
Budleigh Salterton is 11 miles from Junction 30 of the M5 and 4 miles east of Exmouth. The Cosy Teapot is situated at the lower end of the main street, towards the seafront.

Opening times
Open all year except Tuesday and Wednesday. Monday, Thursday, Friday, Saturday, Sunday, 10 am–5 pm in summer, 10 am–4.30 pm in winter.

Local Interest:
Sir Walter Raleigh's birth place is a couple of miles away and Milais' famous painting of Sir Walter on the sea wall is about 50 yards from the shop. The local museum specialises in old lace and there are cliff walks and wonderful surrounding countryside.

This delightful Victorian style tea room is housed in what was once – in about 1880 – the 'Library', and later a shoe-mender's shop. To reach the shop, you have to cross a small bridge that straddles the little stream running right past the door. Once inside, visitors from all over the world enjoy the restful pink, white and burgundy colour scheme, walls decorated with paintings by local artist Eleanor Ludgate, fine Royal Albert china, and a menu that offers sandwiches, toasted sandwiches, soups and salads throughout the day, and a superior range of home-made cakes made locally by talented cooks. At tea-time, there is a Devonshire Cream tea, or as a variation on the traditional theme, the Cosy Teacake Special with a toasted teacake, strawberry jam and clotted cream. And for those who really wish to indulge, the Banana Toastie is a toasted banana sandwich drenched with sugar, topped with caramel sauce and served with clotted cream or ice cream. Popular cakes and desserts include almond and cherry, coffee and walnut, sticky ginger pudding and Cosy Toffee Fudge Surprise. The tea shop also sells a range of teas, farm-made jams and sauces, books, tea-towels and other tea-related items. *Teas served:* Assam, Darjeeling, Earl Grey, Lady Grey, English Breakfast, Lapsang Souchong, Traditional English Afternoon. *Herbal infusions are also offered.*

COURT BARN COUNTRY HOUSE HOTEL

Owners: Susan and Robert Wood

Clawton, Holsworthy
Devon EX22 6PS
Tel: 01409 271219 Fax: 01409 271309

Directions

Clawton is 2 ½ miles south of Holsworthy off the A388 (from Bude to Launceston). Court Barn is next to Clawton's 12th century church.

Opening times
Open all year except the first week of January.
Monday–Sunday, 10 am–5.30 pm.
Bookings preferred for lunch.

Awards
1987 & 89 Tea Council Award of Excellence
Egon Ronay recommended
AA Rosette

Local Interest:
Clawford Vineyard, several local nature trails, Cookworthy Woods, sailing on Roadford and Tomao Lakes, Holsworthy Pannier Market (Wednesday). A short drive to Bude and National Trust beaches and coastal walks.

Court Barn is a charming Victorian House, rebuilt in 1853 from a 16th-century manor house known as Court Baron. The hotel stands in five acres of beautiful tranquil formal gardens hidden amongst rolling Devon countryside and close to the spectacular National Trust and English Heritage coastline.

The house is filled with antiques, paintings and decorative objects. Fresh flowers fill the elegant dining rooms and lounges and there is a crackling log fire in the cosy bar, creating a warm, friendly and relaxed atmosphere. And on balmy summer days, the garden makes an idyllic setting for a special Devon clotted cream tea with one of the 45 teas on the menu. For the more energetic, there is croquet, lawn tennis and badminton or gentle strolls around the garden.

The menu is crammed with wonderful home-baked sweets and savouries, soups and pâtés, vegetarian dishes, sandwiches and cakes such as Marsala and Almond, Honey and Cherry, Chocolate and Walnut. Home cooking at its best! *Teas served:* House Blends (India/Ceylon, India/Kenya), Indian, Darjeeling, Darjeeling and Ceylon, Assam, Kenya, Lapsang Souchong, Earl Grey, Pure China Oolong, Keemun, Rose Pouchong, Gunpowder, Broken Orange Pekoe, English Breakfast. *Fruit flavoured teas and herbal infusions are also offered.*

FOUR & TWENTY BLACKBIRDS

Owner: Jaqueline Webb

43 Gold Street, Tiverton
Devon EX16 6QB
Tel: 01884 257055

Directions

From the M5 take Exit 27, Exeter to Taunton, then take the A373 to Tiverton.

Opening times
Open all year except Sundays.
Monday–Saturday, 9 am–5.30 pm.

Local Interest:
Tiverton's 11th century castle was built by commission of Henry I and the ruins now house the interesting Campbell Clock Collection. The 700 year old church has some beautiful carvings and the award-winning museum contains a lot of railway memorabilia, including the last steam engine to run in the area, affectionately known as the Tivvy Bumper. There are also 11 miles of walks along the banks of the canal and horse-drawn barge rides.

The theme of this totally charming tea shop is the famous nursery rhyme 'Sing a Song of Six Pence'. All the characters from the song are there on the menu – the blackbirds, the King in his counting house, the Queen in the parlour and the maid who was perpetually hanging out the clothes in the garden. The King's choice is savoury – a robust tea with a wholemeal roll, cheddar cheese, chutney and salad – while the Queen delights in sweetmeats and a light tea of boiled egg with bread and butter. The maid's tea is home-made apple pie with clotted Devonshire cream, cheese or ice cream.

Both the outside and inside of the shop (that also sells antiques) are as attrac-tive and appealing as the creative ideas on the menu. The windows – full of porcelain teapots, stoneware jars, jam pots and other tablewares – are dressed with hanging baskets that cascade colour, and once inside, the eye is drawn to lots more interesting objects – baskets, brass trays, decorative plates – that fill the walls and surround the open fireplace. And the array of food on display on the counter and trolley is mouthwatering. Everything is home-made, including the jams, so step into the nostalgic nursery rhyme world of years gone by and indulge in a wonderful traditional tea. *Teas served:* Ceylon, Darjeeling, Assam, Earl Grey, Lapsang Souchong. *Herbal infusions are also offered.*

GREYS DINING ROOM

Owners: David Winstone and Gary Dowland

96 High Street, Totnes
Devon TQ9 5SN
Tel: 01803 866369

Directions
Greys is situated in 'The Narrows' at the top of the High Street opposite the Post Office.

Opening times
Open all year except Wednesdays.
Monday, Tuesday, Thursday and Saturday, 10 am–5 pm. Friday, 9.30 am–5 pm.
Sunday, 12 noon–5 pm.

Awards
1993, 94, 95 & 97 Tea Council Award of Excellence
1996 Tea Council Top Tea Place of The Year
Egon Ronay Recommended

Local Interest:
Totnes has an Elizabethan museum, Norman castle and 17th century Guildhall. Boats go from here to Dartmouth and steam trains will take you up the Dart Valley to Buckfastleigh. From May to the end of September, there is an Elizabethan market every Tuesday in the Market Square and Rotherfold Square.

As you approach the elegant Georgian façade of Greys Dining Room, your eyes are drawn by the old urns in the window that hold graceful ferns. Arranged around them in one window are attractive tablewares and in the other a variety of home-made cakes that invite you to step down into the old world charm of the 250 year old building that once housed an old fashioned sweet shop. Just inside the door, more wonderful cakes are displayed in an antique Flemish glass and wood cabinet carved with cherubs and fruits, that shows the cakes off to perfection, and all around the shop are colourful saucers on the walls, antique furniture, pictures and copper pots and pans.

Surrounded by this classic elegance, treat yourself to tea-time traditionals such as crumpets, toasted teacakes and scones with local Devonshire clotted cream, or a Totnes Tea with two hot buttered crumpets with cheddar cheese and a pot of tea. And then, if you can make up your mind which to choose, indulge in one of the 20 or so cakes. *Teas served:* a range of 40 or more including House Blend, Earl Grey, Darjeeling, Indian Prince, Assam, Keemun, Lapsang Souchong, Ceylon, NAAFI, Lady Grey. *Fruit flavoured teas and herbal infusions are also available.*

THE PARLOUR

Owners: Susan and Philip Hungate

112 East Street
South Molton
Devon EX36 3DB
Tel: 01769 574144

Directions

South Molton is signposted off the North
Devon Link Road that runs off the M5. The

Parlour, with its swinging sign, is on the main
road through the town.

Opening times
Open all year except Sundays and Mondays.
Tuesday–Saturday, 10 am–5 pm. 🚭

Awards
1996 Tea Council Award of Excellence

Local Interest:
South Molton is known for its antique shops selling lace,
pine, paintings, etc, and for the livestock market on
Thursdays and Pannier Market on Thursdays and
Saturdays. South Molton is also a gateway to Exmoor.

As you pass under the traditional fanlight above the doorway of this very attractive double fronted Georgian house, you feel immediately as if you have stepped into Susan and Philip Hungate's front room. A grandfather clock ticks reassuringly in the corner, the walls are deep Georgian green and red and the open fire and warm red of the carpet give a richness and depth to the tearoom. A plate rack runs high up around the walls and displays green Wedgwood plates, and there is an amusing collection of Victorian dolls that was started by Susan and was added to by customers with similar lonely toys.

All the breads, cakes, scones and biscuits are home-made and Susan's range of cakes mixes firm favourites such as apple cake and coffee and walnut with other scrumptious treats such as rich chocolate cake, sticky ginger cake, date and walnut and traditional English cheesecake. Or you can indulge in real traditional tea-time specials such as boiled eggs with soldier boys, cinnamon toast, sardines on toast or real Welsh or Buck Rarebit. A wonderful parlour tea! *Teas served:* Assam, Darjeeling, Earl Grey, Lapsang Souchong, Russian Caravan, Keemun, Jasmine, Uva, Dimbula, Oolong, green Earl Grey, Gunpowder, House English Breakfast Blend.

SALCOMBE REGIS TEA ROOMS

Owners: Patricia and William Davey

Salcombe Regis
Near Sidmouth, Devon EX10 0JH
Tel: 01395 515993
Fax: 01395 577600

Directions
From Exeter, take the Exeter–Lyme Regis Road. Just after Sidford Village turn right at the top of the hill, following signs to Salcombe Regis. The tearooms are on the left as you come into the village.

Opening times
Open all year except January and February. Wednesday–Saturday, 12 noon–6 pm. Sunday, 3–6 pm. Monday and Tuesday, closed.

Local Interest:
Nearby is the wonderful Donkey Sanctuary and Sidmouth Observatory. The tearooms are a short walk from the beach and there are other beautiful walks through preservation areas of outstanding natural beauty.

Teas have been served in Salcombe Regis for over 40 years and Patricia and William are continuing the tradition in their very attractive Grade II early Victorian house. The restaurant is a delightful room with glazed and marble paint effects around the ceiling edges, beautiful colourful curtains, planters filled with flourishing foliage and interesting pictures on the walls. Outside, there is a pretty terrace and garden, with views to the sea, where visitors can dine or take tea on fine summer days. In colder months, the tables close to the gothic log fire indoors are always a favourite spot for hot buttered crumpets and teacakes. For lunch, there are some imaginative and delicious dishes – smoked salmon drizzled with raspberry vinaigrette, duck breasts served warm on a salad with cherry and tarragon dressing, or scallops cooked with fresh herbs and served on a bed of salad with mango. Afternoon tea is just as special, and sandwiches are filled with locally caught crab, or prawn and seafood mayonnaise, wafer thin chicken, tuna and mayonnaise, smoked salmon, or ham and crunchy mustard. And there are home-baked scones with clotted cream and jam, and impossible-to-resist mud pie, lemon cream pie, cheesecake, spicy apple cake, lemon drizzle, chocolate fudge and lots more. *Teas served:* Ceylon, Darjeeling, Earl Grey, Kenya, Summer Tea. *Herbal infusions are also available.*

TETBURY GALLERY TEAROOM

Owners: Jane Maile and
Helen Joyner

**18 Market Place, Tetbury
Gloucestershire GL8 8DD
Tel: 01666 503412**

Directions
Tetbury is ten miles from Junction 17 on the
M4 and ten miles from Cirencester. The
Gallery Tearoom is situated in the centre of
town, just along the road, on the opposite side,
to the pillared Market House.

Opening times
**Open 7 days a week all year except
2 weeks in mid-December.
Times vary according to season.**

Local Interest:
*Walk from the tea shop to the 1655 Market House, the
Georgian Parish Church of St Mary the Virgin with a
spire that is the fourth highest in England. Chipping
Steps was, for centuries, the site of 'Mop Fairs' where
labourers, shepherds and domestic staff sought
employment, and Gunstool Hill is said to have been the
sight of a ducking stool and is today the venue for the
weekly livestock market.*

Tourist guides to the Cotswolds almost run out of superlatives in writing about Tetbury. It is described as a "Cotswold gem", a "superb touring centre", a "most delightful shopping centre" and it is said to have "some of the most handsome rows of houses in the Cotswolds" and to retain "the authentic harmony of a 17th century wool town".

The very centre of town offers a tranquil atmosphere, ancient street names and elegant Georgian façades. Behind one of these, in what was originally the drawing room of an 18th century house, is a tearoom where linen tablecloths, fine bone china and walls hung with fine art combine to recall a more leisurely bygone era. If the weather is fine, there is more seating in a pretty walled courtyard and here you can relax and enjoy some of Jane Maile and Helen Joyner's traditional English home baking. Their cakes and scones are so good that they have been urged to publish a book of recipes, something they are now seriously planning to do. *Teas served:* Breakfast Blend, Earl Grey, Darjeeling, Assam, Ceylon, Lapsang Souchong. *Fruit flavoured teas and herbal infusions are also available.*

THE BATH SPA HOTEL

Manager: Mr Robin Sheppard

Sydney Road, Bath BA2 6JF
Tel: 01225 444424
Fax: 01225 444006

Directions
From London take the M4 and leave at junction 18. Follow the A4 into Bath city centre. At the first set of lights, turn left following signs for A36. Go over Cleveland Bridge and past the Fire Station. At the mini-roundabout, turn right, then next left after the Holbourne Museum into Sydney Place. The Bath Spa Hotel is 200 yards up the hill on the right hand side.

Opening times
Open all year.

Local Interest:
Just over the river are the Abbey, Roman Baths and Pump Room, Costume Museum and No. 1, Royal Crescent, a Georgian house set in the gracious sweep of the crescent, decorated and furnished in period style. The town is full of interesting little streets and alleyways all packed with shops.

The elegance of the city of Bath is recreated in the sumptuous and traditional English style of the Bath Spa. The original mansion, a Grade I listed Georgian building, was built by a General in the Indian army who was renowned for his hospitality. The hotel continues that tradition today and despite its rather grand period style, is extremely welcoming and has a very friendly, comfortable atmosphere.

Guests have a choice of perfect locations for afternoon tea. They can choose the elegant drawing room (once the library), with its sofas, low tables and bookshelves; the muralled colonnade with its ferns and Lloyd Loom chairs and, in summer, the wonderful gardens where tables are set out under large sunshades.

The menu offers a wide selection of equally impressive real food – sandwiches, including toasted and club sandwiches – pastries, biscuits, scones and cakes that are all made in the hotel patisserie. This really is one of the most perfect places to go for afternoon tea. *Teas served:* Darjeeling, Earl Grey, Assam, Lapsang Souchong, Traditional English, Jasmine, Keemun. *Various fruit flavoured teas and herbal infusions are also available.*

THE CANARY RESTAURANT

Owner: Simon Davis

**3 Queen Street, Bath
BA1 1HE
Tel: 01225 424846**

Directions

The Canary is right in the heart of Bath, not far from the theatre. The nearest parking is the Charlotte Street car park.

Opening times

Open all year. Tuesday–Saturday, 9 am–9 pm (May–September, 9 am–10 pm).
Sunday and Monday, 11 am–6 pm.

Awards

1989   Tea Council Top Tea Place of The Year
1988, 89 & 90   Tea Council Award of Excellence
Egon Ronay recommended

Local Interest:

The Pump Room and Roman Baths, the Assembly Rooms, Costume Museum and Royal Crescent are a short walk from Queen Street and all around there are picturesque streets with antique markets and quality shops.

The Canary is in one of Bath's oldest Georgian cobbled streets, tucked away under Trim Bridge where Jane Austen is said to have purchased her hats. When the parents of the present owner, Simon Davis, bought the restaurant in the 1960s, they kept the name but not the birds that had previously sung in their cages there. Mr and Mrs Davis extended into a second Georgian town house next door and created what is today one of the city's most popular restaurants where afternoon tea is a real speciality and the menu includes copious notes and helpful information about the excellent range of more than 40 high quality teas that are offered.

The downstairs rooms have a comfortable traditional feel, while upstairs, light rattan chairs and tables, lots of plants and a mural of nearby Prior Park create a garden atmosphere. Whichever room you choose, sit back and indulge in a freshly baked bagel or granary bread sandwich filled with smoked trout pâté or succulent roast beef, or a wickedly delicious fresh strawberry tea with clotted cream and wholemeal scones. *Teas served:* 10 House Blends, 5 Darjeeling, 2 Assam, 6 Ceylon, 7 China, Formosa Oolong, Earl Grey, Jasmine, Pouchkine. *Flavoured teas and herbal infusions are also offered.*

LEWIS'S TEA-ROOMS

Owners: Ron and Annie Baker

13 The High Street, Dulverton
Somerset TA22 9HB
Tel: 01398 323850

Directions
Dulverton is on the A3223 that runs from
north west to south east across Exmoor.

It is 14 miles north of Tiverton and 25 miles
south of Minehead.

Opening times
Open all year. Times vary according to season.
Monday–Saturday, 10 am–5 pm.
(In summer, 9.30 am–6 pm).
Sunday, 10.30 am–6 pm.
(In summer, 10 am–6 pm). 🚭

Local Interest:
Set on the southern edge of Exmoor, Dulverton is ideally
placed for exploring the area and for visits to Somerset's
coastal towns.

"The quintessential British Tearoom" is how one of the many delighted customers described Lewis's in the visitors' book, and this is exactly what the owners had hoped to create. This bright, spacious tearoom, set in the High Street of this attractive Exmoor town, was originally two rooms and has two fires which burn brightly in winter months. Decorated with pottery, paintings (some by the owner), brush ducks, and small antiques (many of them for sale), this primrose painted room with its wooden floor, floral tablecloths and fresh flowers is instantly welcoming. On sunny days, the small flower-filled courtyard offers the alternative of sitting outside.

Visitors are encouraged by the friendly staff to enjoy a pot of loose leaf tea or a freshly brewed cafetiere of coffee in an unhurried atmosphere, to the background of soothing classical music. As well as the irresistible selection of home-made cakes prominently displayed on the centre table, there is a large choice of cream teas varied according to taste and appetite. Full English breakfasts are also available, alongside a tempting selection of rarebits – firm favourites with the customers – and traditional puddings. *Teas served:* There is a choice of over 20, including *fruit flavoured teas and herbal infusions.*

43

THE PUMP ROOM

Operator: Milburns Restaurants Ltd

Stall Street
Bath BA1 1LZ
Tel: 01225 444477
Fax: 01225 447979

Opening times
**Open all year except Christmas Day and
Boxing Day. April–September 9 am–6 pm.
August 9.30 am–10 pm. October–March,
Monday–Saturday 9.30 am–5 pm,
Sunday 10.30 am–5 pm.**
Closing times may vary slightly.
(Last admission – 30 minutes before closing.)

Directions
The Pump Room is located in the heart of the
City of Bath, adjacent to the Roman Baths, just
50 yards from Bath Abbey.

Local Interest:
*Next door are the famous Roman Baths and close by is the
Abbey, a wide range of museums, Georgian buildings and
other interesting architectural features, shops and antique
markets.*

The historic Pump Room was built by Thomas Baldwin and John Palmer between 1790 and 1795. It overlooks the King's Bath and visitors may taste the Spa waters from Britain's only geo-thermal spring from the Pump Room's Spa Fountain. This magnificent room has been a favourite meeting place since the late 18th century when fashionable society gathered there to socialise and take the waters. Today the room serves as a restaurant that offers elevenses, a selection of excellent hot and cold lunchtime dishes and a full afternoon tea menu. As well as the traditional Pump Room Tea, there is a Champagne Tea with smoked salmon sandwiches, scones with strawberry jam and clotted cream, cakes and pastries and half a bottle of champagne; there is the Tompion Tea (named after the imposing Tompion clock made by the famous clockmaker Thomas Tompion) with a selection of finger sandwiches and home-made scones with jam and cream; and the High Tea which includes cheddar and stilton crostinis and a selection of cakes and pastries. Throughout the day, music is provided by The Pump Room trio or pianist who continue a three hundred year old tradition of music making in these elegant surroundings. *Teas served:* Assam, Ceylon, Darjeeling, Earl Grey, English Breakfast, Lapsang Souchong. *Herbal infusions are also available.*

THE TEA SHOPPE
AND RESTAURANT

Owners: Pam and Norman Goldsack

3 High Street, Dunster
Somerset, TA24 6SF
Tel: 01643 821304

Directions
The Tea Shoppe is situated near the traffic lights in the High Street, by the entrance to Dunster Castle.

Opening times
Weekends (Friday, Saturday, Sunday) in February, November and December. Seven days a week March–end October, 10 am–5.30 pm or later. Friday and Saturday evenings from 7 pm. Closed all January. 🚭

Awards
1989, 90 & 94 Tea Council Award of Excellence
Egon Ronay Award

Local Interest:
Dunster is a medieval town that was once important in the cotton trade. Visit Dunster Castle, St George's Church and Priory, the working water mill and enjoy walks in the surrounding countryside.

Pam and Norman Goldsack came to Dunster from Yorkshire in 1984 and took over the tea shop that had been established here since the 1930s. With a real feel for local specialities, they upgraded it to a restaurant and tearoom and now serve an excellent range of high quality savouries and sweets, including freshly baked rustic breads and cakes made with local produce. The West Country Treacle Tart, Somerset Cider and Bramley Apple cakes are too good to miss, and if you are there for lunch, try the unbelievable bread and butter pudding made with clotted cream – one of 10 or 12 puddings on the menu each day. Pam bakes in an Aga throughout the day and so, at tea time, the scones come to your table as fresh and warm as you will ever find.

The two tearooms are in what were once three little 15th century cottages which retain many of their original features. The roofs are made from the pil reed that grows locally on the Dunster marshes, and the low beams create a comfortable, cottage feel which the Goldsacks have enhanced with country furniture and flowered curtains and wallpaper. The friendly, thoughtful service and delicious food make this a popular venue for visitors from all over the world. *Teas served:* Tea Shoppe Blend, Keemun, Lapsang Souchong, Earl Grey, Darjeeling, Assam, Ceylon. *Fruit flavoured teas and herbal infusions are also offered.*

THE BRIDGE TEA ROOMS

Owners: Francine and Richard Whale

24A Bridge Street
Bradford-on-Avon
Wiltshire BA15 1BY
Tel: 01225 865537

Directions
Turn immediately left after going over the old town bridge and park in the free town car park. Walk out of the car park and the tearooms are situated just across the narrow street in front of you.

Opening times
Open all year except Christmas Day and Boxing Day. Monday–Saturday, 9.30 am–5.30 pm. Sunday, 10.30 am–5.30 pm.

Awards
1994, 95 & 97 Tea Council Award of Excellence
Egon Ronay recommended

Local Interest:
Visit the 12th century Saxon church and the tithe barn with its stone tiled roof that is said to be the largest in England, or walk along the canal and enjoy the undulating surrounding Wiltshire countryside.

Although the building that houses the Bridge Tea Rooms was constructed in 1675, the interior has been themed in Victorian style with aspidistras, 19th century china and memorabilia, including busts of Queen Victoria herself, and sepia photographs of local views and past relatives of the owners, Francine and Richard Whale. The waitresses' costumes recall the early days of London's first tearooms when white frilly aprons were worn over black dresses and white mob caps covered curls and topknots. The ambience and service are delightful, and the food is excellent.

A full afternoon tea includes sandwiches, a crumpet, a scone with thick Devon clotted cream and jam, and a cake. But if you just want a cup of tea and something sweet, there is a wide choice of really luscious cakes and patisseries that come fresh from the oven. Try a slice of carrot, banana and walnut, or choose one of the roulades – Belgian chocolate, fresh strawberry, lemon, hazelnut or pineapple and coconut. *Teas served:* House Blend, Earl Grey, Darjeeling FOP, Assam, Lapsang Souchong, Ceylon BOP, Ceylon Orange Pekoe, Kenya, Pelham, First Flush Darjeeling, Jasmine. *Fruit flavoured teas are also offered.*

POLLY TEA ROOMS

Owner: Julian West

26–27 High Street, Marlborough
Wiltshire SN8 1LW
Tel: 01672 512146

Directions
Marlborough is on the A4. Polly's is half way along the High Street.

Opening times
Open all year.
Monday–Friday, 8.30 am–6 pm.
Saturday, 8 am–7 pm. Sunday, 9 am–7 pm.

Awards
1985   Tea Council Top Tea Place of The Year
Egon Ronay recommended

Local Interest:
The very pretty mainly Georgian High Street is a good hunting ground for antiques and half-timbered houses in some of the back streets are very attractive. St Peter's Church has a craft centre. Nearby, visit Avebury Stone Circle and climb Silbury Hill for panoramic views of the area.

Polly's is probably one of the most important tourist attractions in Marlborough and everyone who has tea here says how wonderful it is. The shop is in a very fine bow-windowed 17th century building that was originally a house and there has been a tea shop here for over 50 years. As you walk through to the large, beamed tearoom, you are bound to be tempted by the mouthwatering array of chocolates and pastries on the counter just inside the entrance. Everything is made on the premises by local pastry chefs and you'll find it hard to decide what to choose from the long list of possibilities – macaroons, rum truffles, date slice, lemon and redcurrant cheesecake, muesli scones, Danish pastries and lots more.

Once you have made your decision, sit back and enjoy the traditional setting with its pretty flowered China, pine dressers, lace tablecloths and neatly uniformed girls who are busy all day serving tourists, schoolboys from nearby Marlborough College and their parents, and local customers who find this the perfect place to sit and relax. *Teas served:* Indian, Earl Grey, Lapsang Souchong. *Fruit infusion is also offered.*

S O U T H   E A S T
R E G I O N A L   M A P

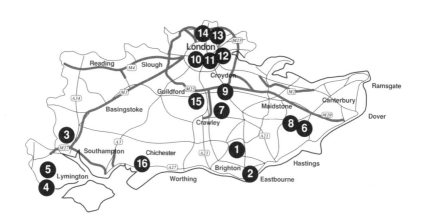

CLARA'S

Owner: Jane Seabrook

9 High Street, East Hoathly
Near Lewes
East Sussex BN8 6DR
Tel: 01825 840339

Directions
East Hoathly is just off the A22 south of
Uckfield. Clara's is in the centre of the village.

Opening times
**Open all year except Mondays, Tuesdays and
two weeks 24th December–mid-January.
Monday–Tuesday, closed.
Wednesday–Saturday, 10.30 am–5 pm.
Sunday, 2–5 pm.**

Local Interest:
*East Hoathly's old petrol station has been converted to
workshops with furniture makers and restorers, a
traditional sign writer, a homeopathic vet, a saddlers and
tack shop, and a carpet warehouse. Also an Antiques
Centre and a shop specialising in products from Gascogne.*

The owner of this pretty tea shop, Jane Seabrook, is very interested in the history of her village and researches the family trees and histories of local village people. East Hoathly was the home of Thomas Turner, diarist and local shopkeeper and Jane sells copies of his writings which chronicle his life in the late 1700s and give a rare and detailed insight into village life in those days. Clara's itself dates from the same period, but has a Victorian facade, and inside, there are oak beams and an inglenook fireplace. In good weather, there is extra seating outside.

Upstairs, there is a very interesting permanent exhibition of knitting, sewing and related memorabilia such as old sewing tools and knitting patterns and the shop sells tapestry kits, knitting yarns, pretty cards, Sussex honey and local home-made chutneys, jams and jellies. The chutney also appears on the menu to accompany delicious rolls filled with chicken, cheese, egg mayonnaise or smoked salmon. The cake selection includes gingerbread, walnut cake and coffee sponge and teas are locally packaged. *Teas served:* Traditional Blend, Earl Grey, Darjeeling. *Herbal infusions are also offered.*

PAVILION TEA ROOMS

Owners: Coastline Caterers on behalf of Eastbourne Borough Council

Royal Parade, Eastbourne
East Sussex BN21 7AQ
Tel: 01323 410374

Directions

The Pavilion Tea Rooms is situated on the seafront, half a mile east of the pier towards the Sovereign Centre.

Opening times
Open all year (except Christmas Day).
In summer, Monday–Sunday, 10 am–9 pm.
In winter, Monday–Sunday, 10 am–5 pm.

Awards
1997 Tea Council Award of Excellence

Local Interest:
Visit the Towner Art Gallery and Museum, the Butterfly Centre on the seafront, the Lifeboat Museum, the Museum of Shops, and the Napoleonic fortress. Also good for walks along the seafront and to Beachy Head.

Pavilion Tea Rooms conjures up images of Victorian and Edwardian tea times at the seaside with pots of Lapsang Souchong or Darjeeling on the terrace while enjoying a stunning vista across the bay to Beachy Head. The setting and the style recreate everyone's idea of all the essential elements of a memorable English tea set amongst the beautiful gardens and croquet lawns – a light and elegant room, waiters who calmly bring you everything you could possibly want, newspapers for browsing through, the gentle sound of the woods from the croquet and the music of the piano on summer afternoons and evenings and winter weekends, and a menu absolutely crammed with wonderful ideas to suit all tastes, at every time of the year, whatever the weather. You may choose to tuck into a cinnamon muffin or nibble at a slice of traditional ginger and walnut cake, dip a long spoon into a raspberry meringue sundae that oozes ice cream, cream, raspberries and topped with a delicious meringue or enjoy an old fashioned cream tea or Pavilion afternoon tea.

Teas served: House Blend, Darjeeling, Earl Grey.

COBWEB TEAROOMS

Owner: Angela Webley

49 The Hundred, Romsey
Hampshire SO51 8GE
Tel: 01794 516434

Directions
Follow signs to Romsey off M27 or M3. Cobweb
Tearooms is the last shop at the end of the main
street, 100 yards from the main entrance to
Broadlands.

Opening times
Open all year except two weeks at the end of
September and one week at Christmas.
Monday and Sunday closed except Bank
Holidays. Tuesday–Saturday, 10 am–5.30 pm.
Bank Holiday Sundays, 2.30–5.30 pm.

Award
1996 Tea Council Award of Excellence

Local Interest:
*From the tea shop, it is only a short walk to Broadlands
(where Lord Mountbatten lived), the Norman abbey, King
John's House and a hunting lodge. Hillier's Arboretum is
three or four miles away and a 15 minute drive south
takes you into the heart of the New Forest.*

The old-world ambience of Cobweb
Tearooms is exactly right for its setting
in Romsey – a charming little town with
interesting antique shops and quaint old
streets on its edges, where Georgian and
Victorian houses stand surrounded by
picturesque gardens. Angela Webley has
established a popular, friendly environment where locals regularly pop in for a
refreshing cuppa after a shopping trip
and where visitors stop off on their way
to the New Forest or after a visit to
Broadlands, the home of Lord Romsey.

The comfortable tearoom is in
a half-timbered, late 17th century building that was once an old-fashioned
cobblers and shoe shop. The outside is
decorated with generously-filled hanging baskets that add a lovely splash of
colour to the white walls. The paved garden at the back provides more seating
and is filled with flowers – a delightful
spot in which to sample some of
Angela's home baking. The trolley is
laden with pavlovas, chocolate hazelnut
torte, carrot cake and chocolate gateau,
and in winter, there are always hot
puds such as sticky toffee pudding
to warm you and fill you up. *Teas
served:* Traditional Typhoo, Nairobi,
Assam, Darjeeling, English Breakfast,
Earl Grey, Lapsang Souchong. *Herbal
infusions are also offered.*

SEA COTTAGE TEA SHOPPE

Owners: Wendy and Kevin Noon

Marine Drive
Barton-on-Sea
Hampshire BH25 7DZ
Tel: 01425 614086

Directions
Travelling south through the New Forest, follow the Lymington road to New Milton where there are signposts to Barton-on-Sea. Keep on this road until you see Sea Cottage Tea Shoppe on the edge of the cliff, overlooking Christchurch Bay.

Opening times
Booking advisable.
Open February–end December. Monday, closed.
Tuesday–Sunday, 10.30 am–5 pm.

Local Interest:
The New Forest and the coastline provide miles of beautiful countryside for walks, cycling and horseriding. Christchurch and Beaulieu are not far away and, to the east, lies Hurst Castle.

Kevin Noon used to serve teas on board the QE2 and this and the marine setting for the cliff-top tea shop has led to a menu with a slightly nautical theme. In the middle of the day, you can feast on the 'Captain's' lunch, and there's a 'Pirates' menu for kids. The cream tea is called 'High Tide' and a set tea of sandwiches and cakes is aptly named 'Full Sail', while 'Half Mast' is scones on their own. Everything is home-made and Wendy and Kevin have won New Forest District Council's awards for their no smoking policy and their healthy cooking. But, don't worry, that doesn't mean that favourite tea-time treats are not available – there are chocolate truffles, apricot and fruit cake, walnut and chocolate sponge and lots more.

Letters of appreciation from past customers bear testimony to the warm welcome, the high standards and friendly service that is given by both Kevin and Wendy. One note says: "We would like to thank you for those excellent lunches, the variety on the menu and not least the happy smiling attention given to us by Wendy. . . . For Kevin, whom we seldom saw, but will be remembered for his culinary skills, our appreciation for all his products." *Teas served:* House Blend, Earl Grey, Darjeeling, Assam, Lapsang Souchong, Lemon, decaffeinated. *Herbal infusions are also offered.*

THATCHED COTTAGE HOTEL & RESTAURANT

Owners: Margaret, Matthias, Martin
and Michiyo Matysik

16 Brookley Road
Brockenhurst, New Forest
Hampshire SO42 7RR
Tel: 01590 623090
Fax: 01590 623479

Directions
Brockenhurst is in the heart of the New Forest
on the A337 and B3055. The hotel is located
on the road into the village centre, a few
minutes walk from the railway station.

Opening times
Open all year except Mondays and 5th–31st
January. Monday, closed. Tuesday–Sunday,
2.30–5 pm. Times vary according to season.

Local Interest:
*The New Forest has facilities for walking, cycling, golf,
horse riding, sailing and fishing.*

The 400 year old thatched cottage was built around the time tea first appeared in England. The Matysik family took over the hotel and tearoom in 1989 and have brought a modern, international flavour to their cuisine, but have kept the old world enchantment and charm. Canaries sing in the tearoom which is filled with antiques, rugs, decorative objects from around the world and arrangements of fresh and dried flowers. The tea garden has cushions, parasols and lace tablecloths to create a sense of luxury and elegance.

Afternoon tea here is a real treat. There is an imaginative and tempting selection of sandwiches, cakes and desserts, ranging from traditional English recipes to foreign specialities such as apple strudel, sachertorte, American cheesecakes and Swiss ice creams. The Complete Cream Tea is incredibly good value and consists of finger sandwiches, three varieties of scone (plain, fruited and wholemeal with walnut) served with very generous portions of jam and clotted cream, a selection of pastries and cakes and a pot of tea. Not surprisingly, people travel from far and wide for such indulgence. *Teas served:* Earl Grey, Assam, Lapsang Souchong, Darjeeling, Pouchkine, Afternoon Dream Tea, decaffeinated. *Fruit flavoured teas and herbal infusions are also offered.*

APPLEDORE TEAROOMS

Owners: Anita and Michael Lucas

8 The Street, Appledore
Kent TN26 2BX
Tel: 01233 758272

Directions

Appledore is situated on the B2080, north east of Rye, south east of Tenterden, and south west of Ashford. From Rye, take the A268 towards London. Turn immediately right on leaving the town and follow the sign to Appledore. The tearooms are at the southern end of the village.

Opening times

Open all year but restricted opening from November–February. Monday, closed. Tuesday–Sunday, 10.30–5.30 pm.

Local Interest:

Close by are Rye, a medieval town steeped in history, Tenterden, a traditional tree-lined Kentish town, Romney Marsh with its many churches, and a historic military canal built in 1805 to repel Napolean in the event of invasion.

Appledore Tearooms' attractive and appealing exterior, with its old-fashioned red telephone box and tubs of plants and flowers, will immediately catch your attention and draw you inside. The small tearoom is housed in part of what was a 16th century long house which was converted in the 17th or 18th century into four cottages. During its history, the building has contained a bakery, a Sunday School, a hospital and even a beer house called 'The Six Bells'. The tearooms' many original features – pretty windows, ornately carved beams and an open coal fire – give it an individual charm. Above the Victorian pine panelling, which lines the walls to dado rail height, hangs a variety of old plates, pictures, tapestries, bread boards and bread knives.

Going in for tea is like entering a private Victorian parlour where visitors can sit back, relax and take tea in a civilised and unhurried manner and where service and value for money are the keywords. Anita's selection of home-made cakes changes daily, but firm favourites are mocha chocolate cake, pecan nut cake and a brandied bread pudding. Cream teas, hot buttered crumpets and muffins are also very popular. After tea, wander through into the adjoining room which is filled with Georgian and Victorian furniture and decorative items. Teas served: House Blend, Assam, Ceylon, Darjeeling, Earl Grey, Lapsang Souchong, China Yunnan, Jasmine. Fruit teas are also available.

Burghesh Court

Owner: Mrs G. M. Everett

3 The Village
Chiddingstone, Edenbridge
Kent TN8 7AH
Tel: 01892 870326
Fax: 01892 870326

Directions
The tea shop is in the centre of Chiddingstone,
which lies between Tonbridge and Edenbridge
on the B2027.

Opening times
11 am–5 pm.
March–September, Tuesday–Sunday.
October–December, Friday–Sunday.
Closed January and February.

Local Interest:
The Village Shop dates back to some time between 1621 and
1636 and has been in uninterrupted business for over 350
years. The Post Office is even older. Chiddingstone Castle is
open to the public and the Chiding Stone is a short walk
away, down a narrow footpath near the school house.

Chiddingstone is one of the prettiest villages in Kent, with its beautiful old timbered Tudor buildings, its authentic Elizabethan atmosphere, its castle and lovely church. Surrounded by some of Britain's most beautiful, gently rolling countryside, the village looks today almost exactly as it did in the reign of Queen Elizabeth I and the tea shop is set in the very heart of one of the most important mansions in the village of that time. Burghesh Court once belonged to a nobleman by the name of Sir Thomas Bullen whose daughter, Ann (Boleyn), became Queen of England and one of Henry VIII's less fortunate wives since she subsequently lost her head for failing to produce a son and heir.

It is the Old Coach House of Burghesh Court that now houses the charming teashop. Here, amidst the rich history of centuries of village life, visitors can take morning coffee, lunch or afternoon tea. The menu offers such traditional treats as toasted teacakes, hot buttered toast and scones with jam and local cream, and the delicious cakes vary according to season. *Teas served:* Earl Grey, Darjeeling, Assam, Lapsang Souchong, Ceylon, Traditional PG Tips. *Herbal infusions are also offered.*

CLARIS'S

Owners: Brian and Janet Wingham

1-3 High Street, Biddenden
Kent TN27 8AL
Tel: 01580 291025

Directions
Biddenden lies at the junction of the A274 and A262, 12 miles south of Maidstone. The tearoom is in the centre of the village opposite the village green.

Opening times
Open all year except Mondays.
Monday, closed.
Tuesday–Sunday, 10.30 am–5.20 pm.

Awards
Egon Ronay recommended

Local Interest:
Within the village, strolling visitors can discover the story of the Biddenden maids who were born joined at the hip and shoulders in 1100 and lived like that for 34 years, refusing to be separated. There are also fine examples of medieval to 17th century architecture and a 13th century church whose school is said to be haunted.

A row of picturesque 15th century weavers' houses graces the gentle bend in the unspoilt main street of this quiet Kentish village that was once the centre of the cloth trade. At the east end of the row stands Claris's tearoom and gift shop with its windows temptingly filled with porcelain and pottery, jewellery and other gifts from the selection inside, and its arched porchway that leads into the old world charm of the shop and tearoom. The low oak beams and the two inglenook fireplaces create an atmosphere of homely cosiness where lace tablecloths cover spacious tables and delicious home-baked cakes and savouries are served on pretty white china.

Having settled at your table, it may take you quite a while to decide between the lemon madeira, the walnut bread served with apricot preserve, the hot bread pudding or Claris's cointreau cake that is covered with oodles of whipped double cream from a local dairy. Or you may decide that a Scottish smoked salmon or prawn sandwich is the ideal accompaniment to your afternoon cup of tea. Whatever you choose, this is the perfect place to relax after a wander around Biddenden village or a ramble in the nearby Wealden countryside. *Teas served:* House Kenya Blend, Earl Grey, Darjeeling, Lapsang Souchong and Assam. *Fruit flavoured teas and herbal infusions are also available.*

ELAN ARTS CENTRE

Owner: Pat Fisher

**Sundridge Road, Ide Hill
Near Sevenoaks, Kent TN14 6JT
Tel: 01732 750344   Fax: 01732 750476**

Directions
Take the M25 to junction 5. Follow signs to Westerham (A25) and at the first set of traffic lights (in Sundridge), turn left into Church Road and continue for about two and a half miles to the top of the hill. Elan is at the roundabout facing the village green and the church.

Opening times
Open mid–February–Christmas Eve.
Monday and Tuesday, closed.
Wednesday–Sunday, 10 am–5.30 pm.

Local Interest:
Ide Hill is a reowned beauty spot, well-known by bikers, hikers, garden enthusiasts and bird watchers. Not far away is Chartwell, Hever Castle, Bough Beach Reservoir, Emmetts Garden and National Trust woodlands at Toys Hill.

Elan Arts Centre is a shoppers' paradise. The spacious 90 year old building, which used to be a grocery store and granary, now houses an ever changing display of paintings and prints by local artists, primarily watercolours featuring Kent's rural charm. There is an exceptionally large selection of fine art greetings cards and unique gift wares from around the world. And when you tire of browsing, the tearoom's hand-made wooden tables provide seating for 32 people in a light airy atmosphere where a further selection of paintings and prints interest the eye while customers enjoy coffee, lunch or tea. In warm, sunny weather, the colourful patio garden full of flowers and hanging baskets provides more space for visitors.

The menu offers an excellent choice of savoury dishes – home-made soups, Elan's ploughmans, pastas, filled jackets – and delicious cakes – Austrian Moist, chocolate fudge, coffee and walnut, lemon layer, orange and elderberry, apple Dorset, carrot with apricot and walnut, toasted teacakes, shortbreads and a selection of white and wholemeal scones (fruit, cheese, apple, walnut and ginger). The home-made jams make cream teas a bonus! *Teas served:* House Blend, Assam, Darjeeling, Earl Grey, Ceylon, Kenya, Lapsang Souchong, decaffeinated. *Herbal and fruit infusions also available.*

THE DORCHESTER

THE PROMENADE

Manager: Mr F. Palminteri

Park Lane, London
W1A 2HJ
Tel: 0171 629 8888
Fax: 0171 495 7351

Directions
The Dorchester is half way up Park Lane.
Nearest tube, Marble Arch.

Opening times
Open all year.
Monday–Sunday, 8 am–1 pm.
Afternoon tea served 3–6 pm.

Awards
Egon Ronay recommended

Local Interest:
Park Lane is very close to Mayfair, Oxford Street
and Hyde Park so there are shops, cinemas, walks,
restaurants and tourist attractions.

Tea at the Dorchester is quite spectacular. No-one can fail to enjoy the elegant, yet leisurely, surroundings where marble pillars, exquisite carpets, stately plants and magnificent flowers in fine vases and planters and amazingly comfortable sofas and armchairs create around you a sense of total calm and refinement. Despite such grand style, the extremely friendly staff make sure you are relaxed and comfortable and have everything you need. The opulence of the occasion recalls the style of the very first Afternoon Teas that took place at the beginning of the 19th century in palaces and stately homes around England.

Tea in The Promenade is brought one course at a time – first the neat finger sandwiches, then the scones with Devonshire clotted cream and jam and finally pastries freshly made by the restaurant's patissier. Second and third servings are always offered but it is doubtful whether many will be able to accept further indulgences. For special occasions, choose a glass of Dorchester champagne to accompany the delicious food. *Teas served:* Dorchester House Blend, Earl Grey, Darjeeling, Assam, China Keemun, Lapsang Souchong, China Caravan, China Oolong, Jasmine, English Breakfast, Russian Caravan. *Fruit flavoured teas and herbal infusions are also offered.*

LE MERIDIEN PICCADILLY

TERRACE GARDEN

Manager: Margaret Paul

21 Piccadilly
London W1V 0BH
Tel: 0171 734 8000
Fax: 0171 437 3574

Directions
Le Meridien Hotel is at Piccadilly Circus, just
along the road from the Royal Academy and
Burlington Arcade. The nearest tube station is
Piccadilly Circus.

Opening times
The Terrace Garden is open all year.
Tea is served every day from 3–5.30 pm.

Local Interest:
*All around Piccadilly and nearby Regent Street, there are
high quality shops, and not far away, Green Park,
Trafalgar Square, the Mall and Buckingham Palace.*

Afternoon tea at Le Meridien has moved from the Oak Room Lounge on the ground floor to the Terrace Garden on the second. As you enter through a stylish bar area, you will be struck by the lightness and elegance of the conservatory-style room arranged on two levels and with a high glass roof and walls. There are plants everywhere – hanging from wrought iron baskets, cascading gently down the walls and decorating every corner and space around the room. High amongst the plants are huge bird cages with ornate fine metal work suspended from the glass ceiling. And the garden feel is enhanced by rattan furniture and vast sunshades, and continues on to the outside balcony where guests may sit in warm weather. Afternoon Tea consists of a carefully devised selection of sandwiches on different breads, warm scones with jams and clotted cream, and delicious little pastries. This really is the most delightful room for tea, and the tranquillity is added to at weekends (and sometimes during the week as well) by the playing of stylish easy-on-the-ear palm court music and favourite tea-time tunes from the Gershwin brothers, Ivor Novello and Irving Berlin by the resident duo. *Teas served:* Assam, Darjeeling, Ceylon, Lapsang Souchong, Keemun, China Oolong, Earl Grey, Jasmine, Gunpowder, Vanilla. *Herbal infusions are also available.*

LE MERIDIEN WALDORF

PALM COURT

Palm Court Manager: Mr Osman El-Tahlawi

Aldwych, London WC2B 4DD
Tel: 0171 836 2400
Fax: 0171 836 7244

Directions
Nearest tube stations are Holborn, Covent

Garden, Temple or Charing Cross. Buses that go to Aldwych are: 1, 9, 11, 13, 15, 23, 26, 68, 76, 77A, 91, 168, 171, 171A, 188, 501, 505, 521.

Opening times
Open all year.
Tea is served Monday–Friday, 3–5.30 pm.
Tea Dances, Saturday, 2.30–5 pm.
Sunday, 3.30–6.30 pm.

Local Interest:
Covent Garden, Royal Opera House, several major theatres, the City of London, and a short walk away over Waterloo Bridge lies the South Bank complex with concert halls, art galleries, theatres and museums.

The Waldorf Hotel opened its doors in 1908 and very quickly became a favourite place for an elegant and refined afternoon tea. In 1910 the Tango arrived from Buenos Aires and prompted the beginning of that rather eccentric mix of Argentine dancing and English tea drinking – the Tea Dance. By 1913, the Waldorf's golden and white ballroom was one of London's most popular venues for Tango Tea Dances.

Today, tea is served in the magnificent Palm Court where exotic plants, a marble terrace, gentle Edwardian colours and twinkling lights create a unique setting for a stylish tea or tea dance. The menu suggests a three course tea with sand-wiches (including prawn Marie Rose on citrus bread, cream cheese and chives with cucumber on raisin and pecan bread, turkey with mustard grain mayonnaise on rye bread), fruit and plain scones, and neat little slices of tiramisu, chocolate mille feuilles, or passion fruit cheesecake. The Friday 'Unlimited Chocolate Buffet' is irresistible to chocolate lovers. Tea Dances are sparkling occasions for both dance and tea enthusiasts. Indulge in slow elegant waltzes, energetic jives and cha cha chas, or the sultry steps of a tango. *Teas served:* Waldorf Blend, Assam, Darjeeling, Ceylon, Earl Grey, Jasmine, Kenya, Lapsang Souchong, mint iced tea. *Herbal infusions are also available.*

LE PAPILLON PATISSERIE

Owners: Chris and Harpal Pollard

249 Muswell Hill Broadway
London N10
Tel: 0181 372 7156

Directions
The nearest tubes are Highgate and East Finchley on the Northern Line, and Bounds Green on the Piccadilly Line. From any of these, the shop is a 5 minute bus ride away. Main bus routes are the 134, 102 and 43.

Opening times
**Open all year except Bank Holidays, Christmas Day, Boxing Day and the last week in August.
Monday–Saturday, 10 am–5 pm.
Sunday, 12 noon–6 pm.**

Local Interest:
Alexandra Palace and Kenwood House are both very near, and 5 minutes away, Highgate Wood, Queens Wood and Hampstead Heath are fantastic for walking.

Harpal and Chris are both exceptionally committed to baking excellent breads, pastries and chocolate specialities. With their particular interest in French patisserie, it was natural, when they decided to expand their bakery to include a tearoom, that it should take on a French atmosphere. Customers used to ask for a place to sit and enjoy some of the wonderful creations, so the tearoom was added upstairs. Now they have extended the tearoom to the ground floor and there is now room for 40 or more people to take lunch or tea. The ambience is exquisite – French chairs, a vast 16th century French painting that creates the focal point upstairs, luxurious orange and white pleated silk curtains bought in Paris, fine white china and friendly, helpful waiters and waitresses. It is so refreshing to find a decor that is so special and elegant and also to be able to enjoy incredibly fine sandwiches, scones (to die for), and absolutely exquisite cakes. Harpal's 'Operas' – neat little slices made of layers of almond sponge, chocolate ganache, coffee butter cream and coffee syrup – are divine. And Chris bakes wonderful flavoured breads, croissants, pains au raisins, and lots more. A fabulous treasure of a tearoom! *Teas served:* Assam, Darjeeling, Ceylon, Earl Grey, Lapsang Souchong, Jasmine. *Herbal infusions are also available.*

THE TEA HOUSE

Owner: Su Russell

College Farm
45 Fitzalan Road
London N3 3PG
Tel: 0171 240 9571
Fax: 0171 836 3893

Directions
The nearest tube station is Finchley Central.
Turn left out of the station, walk to the end of
the road and turn left into Regents Park Road.

Walk about ¼ mile and turn right into Fitzalan
Road. By road, turn off the North Circular
Road at Henlys Corner (junction with Finchley
Road) into Regents Park Road. Fitzalan Road is
off to the left.

Opening times
Open every Sunday, 2–6 pm.
Selected tea parties on other days.
Closed December and January.

Local Interest:
*College Farm still has cattle, sheep, pigs, goats, poultry,
donkeys, etc. Entrance charge: Adults £1.25, Children 70p,
Concessions £1.*

There has been a farm on this site since medieval times. Originally a sheep farm, it was bought in 1868 by the founder of the Express Dairy, G. T. Barham, who redesigned it in 1882 as a working dairy. In 1920, the dairy was turned into a tearoom but sadly, by the early 1980s, had become a rather shabby refreshments room. Then Su Russell became involved and she spent many lonely hours scraping determinedly at the seven layers of paint and paper that concealed the old Minton tiles. Working from a 1920s photograph, she has restored the room to its original charm, with bentwood chairs, chequered floor and tables decorated with linen cloths and fresh flowers.

It has taken Su years to collect the distinctive Willow Pattern tea services and treasures have been given by friends and customers, or hunted out from antique shops. Other 'finds' that add to the feel of nostalgia have been gratefully accepted – Express Dairy tea-towels, an old till and an early ice-cream maker. Now Su serves home-made scones with jam and Devon clotted cream (sent up by train every Sunday from Budleigh Salterton) in this delightful little time warp. *Teas served:* Indian, China, teas from Russia, Malawi, Thailand, Egypt, Singapore, Japan, Zanzibar, decaffeinated. *Fruit flavoured teas and herbal infusions are also offered.*

HASKETTS TEA & COFFEE SHOP

Owner: Emlyn Williams

86 South Street
Dorking, Surrey RH4 2EW
Tel: 01306 885833

Directions
Come into Dorking from the A24 and follow
the High Street until it splits at a Y junction.

Continue up South Street and Hasketts is
the second of two regency bow windowed
buildings on the right, 250 metres from the
Y junction.

Opening times
Open all year except Christmas Day.
Monday–Saturday, 9 am–5 pm.
Sunday, 11.30 am–5.30 pm.

Local Interest:
Loseley Park, the Elizabethan seat of the ice cream
magnate is only a short distance away. Also nearby is
Polesden Lacey, the headquarters of The National Trust.

Hasketts has a home in a Grade II listed building that dates back to 1693. Situated in the sandstone cave district of Dorking, it has a basement that is actually made out of a cave and has a 220 foot well (that is now sealed off). The interior today has a 1920s-30s character and enjoys the impact of all the poster art from that period that decorates the walls. The menu has a similar nostalgia, offering lots of favourite specialities from years gone by, including eggs benedict and corned beef hash, and high tea treats such as ham carved from the bone served with cumberland sauce and a poached egg. There is also an excellent range of sandwiches and salads, and a vast selection of cakes (never less than 24 different varieties), including delicious fruit cakes which are well known abroad through the shop's export business. The tea shop is renowned for its knowledge of and enthusiasm for tea, and for the extensive range of world teas (particularly single source teas) on offer. Emlyn is so keen to share his love of the beverage that he organises educational presentations, and chats willingly to anyone who is interested. *Teas served:* 3 Assams, 3 Darjeelings, 2 Ceylons, English Breakfast, Russian Caravan, Earl Grey, Kenya, China Oolong, Gunpowder, Yunnan, Keemun, Jasmine, Rose Congou, Lapsang Souchong, Japanese, Mate, Rooibos.

SHEPHERDS TEAROOMS

Owners: Yvonne and Richard Spence

35 Little London, Chichester
West Sussex PO19 2PL
Tel: 01243 774761

Directions
Little London is off East Street, one of the
main shopping streets in Chichester.

Opening times
Open all year except Sundays.
Monday–Friday, 9.15 am–5 pm.
Saturday, 8 am–5 pm. Sunday, closed.

Awards
1989, 91, 93, 96, 97 Tea Council Award of Excellence
1990, 92, 95 Tea Council Top Tea Place of The Year
Egon Ronay recommended 94, 95, 96

Local Interest:
*The medieval city walls, the Market Cross of 1501, the
Cathedral, Chichester District Museum and the Guildhall
are all within walking distance of Shepherds. Also nearby,
the remains of a magnificent Roman villa at Fishbourne
to the south west of the city.*

Housed in a fine Georgian listed building, Shepherds has a calm, friendly, living-room atmosphere and efficient, attentive waitresses. Floral curtains, ivory walls and rich red tablecloths covered with lace set a traditional theme and the room is decorated with plants and dried flowers and there are vases of fresh flowers on the tables. The windows of the conservatory at one end flood the room with light and warmth and make this a very popular, restful venue for tourists, local business people and weary shoppers who tuck into tasty rarebits, sandwiches and scrumptious sweet treats such as Earl Grey and Sultana Cake or Coffee and Walnut Sponge. The traditional cream tea with home-baked scones and generous portions of jam and cream are well worth a special visit.

Since 1987 when they acquired the tearooms, Yvonne and Richard Spence have constantly set very high standards and have researched different blends and suppliers of tea in order to offer only the best. Their special blends are so popular that they are now available by mail order or from the small shop. *Teas served:* English Breakfast, Ceylon Afternoon, Darjeeling, China Black, Earl Grey, Assam, Gunpowder, Jasmine. *Fruit flavoured teas and herbal infusions are also offered.*

E A S T

R E G I O N A L   M A P

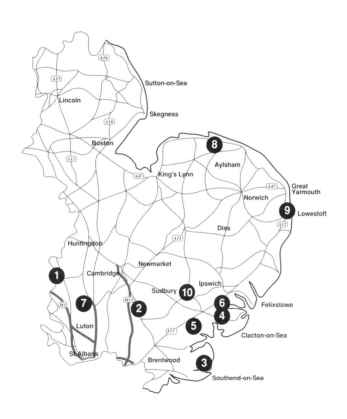

THE TEA ROOM

Owner: Barbara Johnson

9 East Street, Kimbolton
Cambridgeshire PE18 0HJ
Tel: 01480 860415

Directions
Kimbolton lies on the B645 between
Cambridge and Northampton. The tea shop is
at the east end of the village.

Opening times
Open April–mid-December.
Closed mid-December–end March.
Saturday, 10.30 am–5.30 pm.
Sunday, 1.30 pm–5.30 pm.
Monday–Friday, closed. 🚭

Awards
Egon Ronay recommended

Local Interest:
Kimbolton Castle was built in the early 1600s and
Catherine of Aragon, Henry VIII's first wife, lived the last
18 months of her life there after having been exiled by the
King. The 15th century church is also worth a visit.

Barbara Johnson first thought of opening a tea shop in 1947 when she was personally trained by Lord Forte while working in a milk bar that he then owned in Brighton. The ambition surfaced again while very successfully running her house in Kimbolton as a Bed and Breakfast guest house and now visitors are stunned by the magic of the tearoom. For it is not just a house, it is a medieval hall with stone-tiled floors, wonderful low beams and a courtyard in York stone and with high old red brick walls covered with ivy and hanging flower baskets. The tearoom has just been enlarged to seat more eager customers and soon the garden will have the added charm of a fountain.

What could be more appropriate than to relax in the delightful garden or tearoom and tuck into one of Barbara's delicious cakes. There's a chocolate and raspberry roulade, a coffee chiffon cake with coffee cream and pecan nuts, or a light-as-air angel cake with strawberries, cream and raspberry sauce. Or you may indulge in a traditional cream tea or add a touch of summer luxury by adding fresh strawberries to the scones, jam and cream. *Teas served:* Earl Grey, Assam, Darjeeling, Lapsang Souchong, Coop 99 Tea. *Fruit flavoured teas are also offered.*

THE CAKE TABLE TEAROOM

Owners: Kathleen and Robert Albon

5 Fishmarket Street, Thaxted
Essex CM6 2PG
Tel: 01371 831206

Directions
Thaxted is well signposted on the B1051
and B184. The tearoom is tucked away to
the left of the Guildhall.

Opening times
Open all year during winter months except for
Christmas and Annual Holidays. Monday,
closed. Tuesday–Sunday, 11 am–5 pm.
Open Bank Holidays. Please telephone for
winter mid-week opening hours.

Awards
1990 & 97   Tea Council Award of Excellence
1991   Tea Council Top Tea Place of The Year
1993–96   Egon Ronay recommended

Local Interest:
Thaxted Guildhall was built in 1390. The town
is also famous for its medieval church and windmill.

One of Kathleen Albon's customers recently described her visit to The Cake Table as "just like being at home". The Albons have certainly achieved a very homely, old-fashioned atmosphere, with old beams, chintz curtains and furnishings, white china, an open fire, classical music and lots of really good home baking – coffee and walnut, traditional bread pudding and the scones being the most popular. The interior is so traditionally English and attractive that film crews have used the tea shop as the setting for television dramas and the stars have themselves stopped for tea.

Kathleen serves a very interesting range of well-known and more obscure teas from around the world. The menu gives valuable information about the taste and benefits of these and some, displayed on the dresser, are for sale. The shop also sells tea cosies, locally made hand-smocked aprons and floral prints by a local artist. In good weather, there is additional seating in the pretty walled garden where hanging baskets continue the theme of old world charm. *Teas served:* House Blend, Assam, Darjeeling, Earl Grey, English Breakfast, Keemun, Kenya, Lapsang Souchong, Yunnan, Russian Caravan, Oolong, Gunpowder, Japanese Sencha, Lychee, decaffeinated, organic, iced tea on summer days. *Fruit flavoured teas and herbal infusions are also offered.*

THE CROOKED COTTAGE TEA ROOMS

Owner: Anne Woolfson

1 The Quay, Burnham-on-Crouch
Essex CM0 8AS
Tel: 01621 783868
Fax: 01621 783868

Directions
There is pedestrian access only. Walk down the High Street until you see, on the right, a restaurant called Simply Red. A pathway to the side leads to the Tearooms. There is also access from the river front.

Opening times
Open March–October and weekends only 1st November–1st March. Monday, closed except Bank Holidays. Tuesday–Sunday, 10 am–5 pm. Sunday lunch is a speciality.

Local Interest:
The quaint little sailing town has a marina, a clock tower, fresh shellfish stalls by the war memorial and wonderful walks along the waterside.

This very crooked cottage is over 300 years old and was once a fisherman's home. There are boatyards on either side and a dock and the tearoom has a wonderful view over a picturesque stretch of the river with its steady stream of fishing boats and yachts. The outside of the interesting little house is covered with white weatherboards and the inside of the oak-beamed room is filled with ornaments and decorative objects and lots and lots of pictures of cats, for the owner of the tearoom, Anne Woolfson is a dedicated cat-lover.

In summer there are ten tables in the charming secluded cottage garden where a pond with fish, a rockery, a sundial, old-fashioned roses and lots of colourful flowers blend all the elements of the perfect traditional English garden. There is an excellent selection of traditional home-baked goodies on the menu, too, and with one of 18 different teas, you can enjoy scones, cinnamon toast, marmite soldiers, gingerbread men and luscious cakes that include hot Devon Apple Cake covered with cream. On sale also is a range of the famous locally-made Burnham mustard, mustard pots, jams and a speciality salad dressing called Burnham Mud! *Teas served:* Ceylon, Assam, Kenya, Darjeeling, Earl Grey, China Jasmine. *Fruit flavoured teas and herbal infusions are also offered.*

POPPYS TEA ROOMS

Owners: Anthony and Anita Benton

**17 Trinity Street, Colchester
Essex CO1 1JN
Tel: 01206 765805**

Directions
Take the A12 from the M25 and follow to Colchester. Poppys is in the town centre next to the Clock Museum.

Opening times
**Open all year.
Monday–Thursday, 9.30 am–5 pm.
Friday and Saturday, 9.30 am–5.30 pm.
Sunday, closed.**

Awards
Egon Ronay recommended

Local Interest:
Poppys is set in the old part of Colchester that has not been spoilt by large modern buildings. It is surrounded by narrow streets and Roman ruins. Colchester is Britain's oldest recorded town.

Poppys gets a lot of visits from foreign tourists and one group wrote in the guest book, "We didn't expect such big meals in such a small restaurant – we will be back!" It is small, but its large reputation as being the best in Colchester has spread beyond the immediate locality because of its charming Victorian style and the delicious food. The building is full of old beams and Victorian bric-a-brac, including pots and pans around the hearth, a spinning wheel and antique crockery stacked on dressers, and the staff wear period uniforms with mob caps.

As well as a very wide range of all day dishes – quiches, hot jacket potatoes, pastas and pies – there is an excellent choice of hot and cold sandwiches – honey roast ham with pickle, prawn mayonnaise, roast beef and mustard, pork sausage, BLT, beef and bacon, and even roast beef and gravy. And, for the health conscious, the menu includes large helpings of seasonal mixed salads and home-made soups. Tea-time brings four set menus with sandwiches, scones, croissants, crumpets, teacakes, and a whole host of cakes and puddings known as Poppys Pudding Club! *Teas served:* Darjeeling, Earl Grey, English Breakfast, Yorkshire. *Fruit flavoured teas and herbal infusions are also available.*

THE TEA ROOM

Manageress: Colette Harrington

**Wilkin & Sons Ltd
Tiptree, Essex CO5 0RF
Tel: 01621 815407   Fax: 01621 819468**

For group bookings, please telephone
Angela Marris on 01621 815407.

Directions

**Leave the A12 at Kelvedon and take the B1023
to Tiptree (4 miles). Cross the B1022 into
Tiptree Village heading for Tollesbury. As you**
leave the village, Wilkin & Sons is immediately
on the right. The entrance to the tearoom is 200
metres further on, on the right, well signposted.
If lost ask for 'the jam factory'.

Opening times
June–late August, open 7 days a week,
10 am–5 pm. End of August–end of May, open
Monday–Saturday, 10 am–5 pm. Closed Sunday.

Local Interest:
*Close by, there are Pick-Your-Own fruit farms, the River
Blackwater for fishing and sailing, the riverside town of
Maldon, Chappel Steam Railway Museum, Layer Marney
Towers (a historic house), Colchester, the oldest recorded town
in Britain, Colchester Zoo, and various parks and gardens.*

Wilkin & Sons Tiptree Tea Room is
located in an old building on their fruit
farm, right next door to the famous jam
factory. Surrounded by the fruit fields
that made Tiptree famous, the tearoom
is an ideal place to spend an hour over
afternoon tea after a leisurely walk
through the local countryside or along
the sea wall at nearby Tollesbury. Or
you might prefer the peace and solitude
of a walk along the tow path of the old
Chelmer and Blackwater Canal, just 10
minutes drive from Tiptree.

The tearoom seats 90 and welcomes
coach parties for special visits and birth-
day teas and anniversaries. The menu
offers a range of quality sandwiches and
home-made scones and cakes, such as
lemon meringue pie and walnut cake.
The speciality is the cream tea served
with Tiptree's delicious and daintily
named 'Little Scarlet' preserve – appar-
ently James Bond's favourite jam which
is on sale all year round in the Jam Shop.

112 years after the first jam was
made at Tiptree, Wilkin & Sons is still a
family business, and the great grandson
of the founder, Peter Wilkin, is the present company chairman. *Teas served:*
Assam, Darjeeling, Ceylon, Earl Grey.

TRINITY HOUSE TEAROOM & GARDEN

Owners: Ray and Heather Ablett

47 High Street, Manningtree
Essex CO11 1AH
Tel: 01206 391410
Fax: 01206 391216

Directions
Take the A137 from Ipswich, or the A131 from Colchester into the centre of Manningtree. Trinity House is situated in the main street.

Opening times
Open all year, including Bank Holidays. Monday–Friday, 9 am–5 pm. Saturday in winter, 9 am–5 pm. Saturday in summer, 9 am–6 pm. Sunday in winter, 1 pm–5 pm. Sunday in summer, 1 pm–6 pm.

Local Interest:
The tearoom overlooks the River Stour with its boating area, also close by are The Walls, a grassed walking area along the river - a good point from which to view birds and wild fowl and a favourite spot for artists.

Trinity House Tearoom is run to help support and provide work for the residents of Acorn Village – a community within Manningtree for people with learning disabilities. A great deal of care and thought goes into the organisation of the tea shop and its menu. Trinity House holds the local council's Hygiene Award for healthy living and healthy options include all sorts of lunchtime savoury dishes, filled rolls and sandwiches. There's a tempting array of home-made cakes (including indulgent treats such as lemon meringue pie with cream, Danish pastries and fruit pies with custard, ice cream or cream) and fat free teabreads and sponge cakes.

The tearoom is on the scenic Coastal Route from Harwich, in a prime position in the heart of Manningtree (said to be the smallest town in Britain) with a perfect view of the River Stour that runs alongside the village. It's a popular stop for cyclists and has parking nearby. The beautiful Tea Garden is entered each year in the local Floral Manningtree Competition in conjunction with Anglia in Bloom. *Teas served:* A very wide variety including House Blend, Yorkshire Blend, Assam, Earl Grey, Lady Grey, Darjeeling, Lapsang Souchong, English Breakfast, decaffeinated, iced teas. *Fruit flavoured teas and herbal infusions are also available.*

E A S T

THE TEA & COFFEE HOUSE

Owner: Shirley Davies

6/7 Market Place
Hitchin, Herts SG5 1DR
Tel: 01462 433631

Directions
The Tea & Coffee House is located in the town centre on the Market Place Square.

Opening times
Open all year except Sunday.
Monday–Saturday, 9.30 am–5.30 pm with last orders taken at 5 pm.

Awards
1997 Tea Council Award of Excellence

Local Interest:
Hitchin is a beautiful market town. Many local features include an open market on Tuesday, Friday and Saturday; a Victorian chemist shop housed in the museum; and a physic garden alongside.

The Tea & Coffee House is a privately owned business which started as a shop selling specialist teas and coffees in 1986. In 1993, the business moved to larger premises where a seating area serving teas and coffees was created alongside. In May 1996 the business again expanded to its new central location and now offers the customer a sense of space and light with huge picture windows overlooking the main market square. Classical music is played and the daily papers are provided for customers' enjoyment.

The range of teas gives an almost unique opportunity for customers to sample and buy really unusual blends and speciality teas and coffees.

The food is of as high a quality as the beverages with all food freshly prepared to order and all cakes home-made.

The staff are extremely helpful with advice about which tea to order, and, when you have found one you like, you can buy more from the counter to take home or give as a gift. *Teas served:* 70 different varieties including a House Blend (Assam & Kenya), Darjeeling, Assam, Ceylon, Kenya, China Silver Tip Oolong, Ceylon, African, China, Japanese, decaffeinated and exotic flavoured teas. *Fruit flavoured teas and herbal infusions are also available.*

Margaret's Tea Rooms

Owners: Margaret and Roger Bacon

**Chestnut Farmhouse, The Street
Baconsthorpe, Near Holt, Norfolk
NR25 6AB
Tel: 01263 577614**

Directions
400 yards from the Holt–Norwich (B1149)
roundabout is the road to Baconsthorpe. Stay
on this road for 3 miles and you will come
straight to Margaret's Tea Rooms (300 yards
from the village Post Office).

Opening times
10.30 am–5 pm, Good Friday to end October,
Tuesday–Sunday. Closed Monday except
Bank Holidays.

Award
1997 Tea Council Award of Excellence

Local Interest:
*The ruins of Baconsthorpe Castle are less than 5 minutes'
walk away and a short drive takes you to Sheringham
and the North Norfolk coast with its beaches and bays.
Nearby Holt is an extremely interesting Georgian town
with very attractive shops.*

Margaret and Roger Bacon's mid-17th century farmhouse is a warm, welcoming home, with guest bedrooms and two tea-rooms – the Harebell and Strawberry parlours. Lace tablecloths and themed china enhance the traditional settings, and in the colder months, a wood burning stove in the Harebell, and the oak surround open fire in the Strawberry add to the warm ambience.

Margaret's home cooking makes every visit special. She makes all the breads, cakes, biscuits, scones, soups, jams and pickles herself in the farmhouse kitchen. Daily choices may include delicious pies and quiches, familiar favourites such as carrot cake, coffee and walnut, hot marmalade bread pudding with cream, and different sorts of shortbread. Or sample her more unusual surprise tart. The cream teas are a must – plain scones with home-made jam and fresh double cream from the local dairy.

While Margaret is busy baking, her husband, Roger, is making solid wood furniture in his workshop, and photographs and samples of his work can be seen in the house. *Teas served:* House Blend, Earl Grey, Darjeeling, Assam, Ceylon, Nilgiri, Lapsang Souchong, Rose Pouchong, Oolong, Keemun, Yunnan, Gunpowder, Jasmine, Russian Caravan, English Breakfast, Rwanda, iced tea. *Herbal infusions are also available.*

FLYING FIFTEENS

Owners: Peter and Diana Knight

19a The Esplanade, Lowestoft
Suffolk NR33 0QG
Tel: 01502 581188   Fax: 01502 581188

Directions
The tea shop is located on the seafront
promenade of the South Beach between the
two piers near to the Hatfield Hotel.

Opening times
January–March, closed
April–Mid-May and October–December, open
some weekends, times dependent on weather.
(Please telephone before visiting.)
Mid-May–the end of September, open
Tuesday–Sunday, 10.30 am–5 pm.
Closed Monday, except Bank Holidays.

Local Interest:
Lowestoft's South Beach has been awarded the title of
'Best Beach in England'. It is cleaned daily and dogs are
banned. The Royal Norfolk and Suffolk Yacht Club is
also close by.

The unusual name for this delightful tearoom comes from the Flying Fifteen sailing boats that can regularly be seen racing out of the nearby Yacht Club. The boat was designed by Uffa Fox in 1947 and in his book 'Sailing Boats' there is an interesting account of how he took Prince Philip's Flying Fifteen 'Cowslip' to the 1958 Lowestoft June Regatta.

A great deal of thought has gone into the design of the tearoom and the light decor of pale yellow and pale turquoise reflects the colours of sea and sand so that visitors both inside and out, in the pretty garden that adjoins the seafront, can enjoy a seaside atmosphere.

The menu is similarly very carefully put together and everything is beautifully presented on china designed by Jeff Banks. Sandwiches are filled with locally produced ham or smoked salmon, the scones draw compliments all the time from impressed customers and the home-made cakes are always popular – especially the boozy fruit cake, made with fruit steeped in beer. Although only opened in 1996, and despite very little advertising, Flying Fifteens is rapidly, and quite rightly, gaining a reputation for delicious food and excellent service. *Teas served:* Assam, Darjeeling, English Breakfast, Earl Grey, Ceylon.

THE SWAN

Manager: Elizabeth Combridge

High Street, Lavenham
Sudbury, Suffolk
CO10 9QA
Tel: 01787 247477
Fax: 01787 248286

Directions
Lavenham is on the A1141 between Bury
St Edmunds and Hadleigh. The Swan is

located in the centre of the medieval village
of Lavenham.

Opening times
Open all year.
Tea is served in the lounge from
3 pm–5.30 pm.

Local Interest:
*In the Middle Ages, Lavenham was the centre of the wool
trade and one of the wealthiest towns in England. Walk
from The Swan to the medieval Guildhall (National
Trust), the Priory, the Little Hall and the cathedral-like
Church of St Peter and St Paul.*

In the 15th century, four timbered houses in the centre of this incredibly unspoilt and picturesque town were united to form the Swan Hotel and today it is still a hotel of great character and charm and a perfectly wonderful place to stop for a traditional English tea. The cosy, comfortable lounge has quaint snug corners that are ideal for a quiet, refined cup of tea, open fireplaces where roaring log fires crackle their welcome in winter months, generous arrangements of fresh and dried flowers all over the room and a lovely view of the walled, cloistered garden with its lawn surrounded by pretty borders. In summer, customers spill out into this beautiful space for their three course tea that is served on silver, tiered cake stands, or a cream tea with home-baked scones, home-made jams and Cornish clotted cream.

At weekends, the old-world atmosphere of refinement and gentle pleasure is enhanced by harpsichord recitals. You will feel as if you have settled into a genteel country house where afternoon refreshment is an essential part of each day's enjoyment. *Teas served:* House Blend, Earl Grey, Assam, Darjeeling, Lapsang Souchong.

MIDDLE ENGLAND
REGIONAL MAP

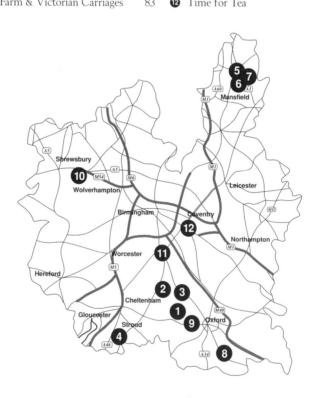

BO-PEEP TEA ROOMS AND RESTAURANT

Owners: Angela and Hugh Holloway

**Riverside, Bourton-on-the-Water
Cheltenham, Gloucestershire
GL54 2DP
Tel: 01451 822005**

Directions
Bourton-on-the-Water is situated just off the A429 between Stow-on-the-Wold and Cirencester. Park in the main car park, cross the High Street and turn right. The footbridge adjacent to the road bridge takes you over the river and directly to the tearooms.

Opening times
Open all year. Monday, Tuesday, Friday, Saturday, Sunday, 9 am–9 pm. Wednesday and Thursday, 9 am–5.30 pm.

Awards
1992, 93, 94 & 96 Tea Council Award of Excellence
Egon Ronay recommended

Local Interest:
There is a model of the village in the garden of The New Inn, a model railway, an exhibition of perfumerie, Birdland (a collection of 600 different species of birds) and a motor museum.

What could be a more perfect setting for tea than a garden seat beside the River Windrush as it flows gently through the middle of this very pretty Cotswold village, under elegant low stone 18th century bridges and alongside immaculate gardens with their neat lawns and colourful flower borders.

Bo-Peep Tea Rooms is in the ideal location and offers an excellent range of breakfast, lunch, tea-time and evening dishes to suit everyone, including those who prefer low fat, high fibre and vegetarian dishes, for the restaurant holds a Heartbeat Award for its healthy options. The menu tempts visitors with all sorts of traditional treats – sandwiches filled with prawns, ham, tuna, cottage cheese or cucumber, and toasted teacakes, scones, pastries, shortbreads and flapjacks, as well as ice creams, yoghurts and more indulgent puddings and desserts. The list of more than 30 teas offers a comprehensive selection from around the world and, to help less experienced tea drinkers, the menu very thoughtfully indicates the strength of the different teas with a rating scale from 1 to 8. *Teas served:* Assam, Ceylon, Nilgiri, Darjeeling, Earl Grey, English Breakfast, Afternoon Tea, Kenya, Russian, Lapsang Souchong, Keemun, Gunpowder, Japanese Sencha. *Flavoured teas and herbal infusions are also available.*

Forbes Brasserie at the Cotswold House

Owners: Christopher and Lousie Forbes

**The Square, Chipping Campden
Gloucestershire GL55 6AN
Tel: 01386 840330   Fax: 01386 840310**

Directions
Chipping Campden is on the B4081, one mile north of the A44, between Broadway and Moreton-in-Marsh. Forbes is in the centre of town, next to the Cotswold House Hotel.

Opening times
**Open all year except 23rd–26th December
Monday–Sunday, 9.30 am–11 pm.
Teas are served from 3–6.30 pm.**

Local Interest:
The area has a large number of historic buildings (Snowshill Manor, Ragley Hall), ancient castles (Sudely, Berkeley, Warwick) and world famous gardens (Hidcote, Kiftsgate). This is an excellent base for walks in the Cotswolds.

The Cotswold House has pride of place on the sunny side of Chipping Campden's medieval Market Square. The beautiful regency building of Cotswold stone is Campden's leading award-winning hotel and Forbes, one of the hotel's two restaurants, is the perfect place to stop for tea. The setting is charming and stylish and the food delicious. Tea is served every day in what was originally the ground floor of three little houses dating back to 1650. The classic green and rich burgundy decor is complemented by 40 original photographs of Chipping Campden dating from 1850 to 1930. French doors open to a delightful paved courtyard for alfresco dining under the shade of willow and fig trees in the summer air.

Forbes is justly proud of its service and the quality of its food, and everything on the menu – including the renowned Danish pastries, delicious cheese scones and the huge bacon, lettuce and tomato sandwiches – is freshly made on the premises. *Teas served:* House Blend, Assam, Ceylon, Darjeeling, Earl Grey, Lapsang Souchong, Orange Pekoe, Chrysanthemum, iced tea (in summer). *Fruit flavoured teas and herbal infusions are also offered.*

The MARSHMALLOW

Owner: Valerie West

High Street, Moreton-in-Marsh
Gloucestershire GL56 0AT
Tel: 01608 651536

Directions
Moreton-in-Marsh is on the A429 between
Stratford-upon-Avon and Stow-on-the-Wold. The
tea shop is at the north end of the town, in the
main shopping street, not far from the station.

Opening times
Open all year. Monday, 10 am–5 pm. Tuesday,
10 am–4 pm. Wednesday–Saturday, 10 am–
9.30 pm. Sunday, 10.30 am–9.30 pm.

Awards
1996 Tea Council Award of Excellence

Local Interest:
*The High Street in which the Marshmallow stands was part
of the Roman Fosse Way that ran from Devon to the north
east of England. All around the town there are examples of
typical Cotswold houses with their steeply pitched roofs.
Also, lots of antique shops and the Wellington Art Gallery
for those interested in paintings of aircraft.*

Having never been involved in catering before acquiring this lovely Grade II
listed building, Valerie West now runs a
thriving restaurant and tearoom right in
the heart of the busy town that was
once very important in the wool trade.
Within ten days of moving in, Valerie
had rebuilt and opened her 96 seat dining room and is busy all year with
tourists, regular customers and passing
visitors, particularly on Tuesdays when
the traders' market comes to town.

The front of the building is covered
with Virginia Creeper and in the flag-
stoned courtyard at the back, where
more tables and hanging flower baskets
create a very restful place in which to sit
and have tea. Waitresses are dressed in
gentle shades of peach and pale green,
furnishings are pine, set against original
stone walls, and there is a view through
to the homely kitchen where copper
pots and pans decorate the walls and the
chefs create wonderful cakes and
savouries. The cake trolley is laden with
truly delicious creations – chocolate
mousses, roulades, mille feuille gateaux,
pecan Danish pastries and so much more
to tempt you. *Teas served:* House Blend,
Earl Grey, Assam, Lapsang Souchong,
Darjeeling, Traditional. *Fruit flavoured teas
and herbal infusions are also offered.*

TWO TOADS

Owners: Andrew Dawes and
Wendy Rochefort

19 Church Street
Tetbury
Gloucester GL8 8JG
Tel: 01666 503696

Directions
Two Toads is located on the Bath Road that
runs from Bath to Cirencester. As you come

into the village, the shop is half way between St
Mary's Church and the Town Hall.

Opening times
Open all year except Christmas.
Monday–Saturday, 9.30 am–5 pm.
Sunday, 10.30 am–4.30 pm.

Local Interest:
*In the village, visit St Mary the Virgin church and Chipping
Steps. And nearby is Prince Charles' home, Highgrove, and
Westonbirt, a private girls' school where the gardens and
arboretum are open to the public.*

Andrew and Wendy both gave up their jobs – Andrew as a nuclear engineer and Wendy as an office administrator – to open Two Toads and say they have absolutely no regrets. The building in which they have created this bright sunny yellow tearoom was built in 1675 and the middle section was once a barn. The decor is light and fresh, with pale ash bentwood furniture, flowers on the tables, country and garden prints on the walls (some for sale by local artists), waitresses' aprons in green and black stripes over black uniforms and calm, elegant, easy music of the 1920s and 30s. In the beautiful courtyard garden at the back, a very popular spot for up to 30 guests in summer, there is a cherry tree, rose arch, and borders and tubs filled with plants and flowers.

The menu lists soups and jacket potatoes, pasties and quiches, filled baguettes and fresh cut sandwiches served with mixed salad leaves, and several of the products used – the cheeses, ham and fruit juices – come from local award winning suppliers. For tea-time, order Devon clotted cream to eat with scones and jam, or try the scrumpy cider cake or Cotswold cookies flavoured with coconut and ginger. *Teas served:* House Morning Blend, Assam, Ceylon, Darjeeling, Earl Grey, Lapsang Souchong, China Oolong, Yunnan, Gunpowder, Jasmine.

OLDE SCHOOL TEAROOM

Owner: Gwen Elliott

**Carburton, Near Worksop
Nottinghamshire S80 3BP
Tel: 01909 483517**

Directions
Carburton is on the B6034 that runs from
Worksop to Allerton. The Olde School
Tearoom is at the crossroads with the road that
runs from Clumber Park to Norton village.

Opening times
Open all year except January and Mondays.
Monday, closed.
Tuesday–Friday, 10 am–4.30 pm.
Saturday and Sunday, 10 am–5 pm.

Award
1992   Tea Council Award of Excellence

Local Interest:
*The Olde School is opposite one of the entrances to
Clumber Park and as Carburton is in the middle of
Sherwood Forest it is an excellent area for walks. At
nearby Edwinstow is the Sherwood Forest Visitor Centre
and at Newark, an interesting castle.*

Many of the regular customers in this converted 1930s school are local people who love the peace and quiet of a country tearoom. But it is also an ideal place for tourists after a drive or ramble in Sherwood Forest or Clumber Park. Gwen Elliott has preserved the spirit of the school building and has an old school desk in the entrance, her menu written up on the blackboard and easel and the original children's hand basins in the wash rooms. The old school shelves, once used for reference books and stacks of homework, now display woodwork, greeting cards and handmade prints by local artists. The partition that in the past divided the main classroom into two is now used to make a separate room for private parties, and the old school bell is still available to attract the attention of large groups if they are being too jolly and making too much noise!

Good service and value are important to Gwen and her menu offers a very reasonably priced selection of home-made savouries and cakes and freshly cut sandwiches. The most popular cake is something her mother used to make when Gwen was a child – a fruit slice with a pastry base, a layer of jam and topping of sponge full of dried fruits. *Teas served:* House Blend, Assam, Darjeeling, Earl Grey, Ceylon.

OLLERTON WATER MILL TEA SHOP

Owners: Kate and Ellen Mettam

Ollerton Mill, Market Place
Ollerton, Newark
Nottinghamshire NG22 9AA
Tel: 01623 824094/822469

Directions
Ollerton lies at the junction of the A614 and
B616, between Worksop and Nottingham. The
Water Mill and Tea Shop are in the centre of
the village, almost opposite the church.

Opening times
Open March–mid November. Tuesday–Sunday,
10.30 am–5 pm. Open every Bank Holiday and
any other time by arrangement.

Awards
1994 & 95   Tea Council Award of Excellence

Local Interest:
*The mill has an exhibition with colourful display panels
which tell the story of the mill. There is also a video which
shows the mill grinding and producing flour.*

Ollerton is situated on the edge of Sherwood Forest in a corner of rural England that has remained unchanged for three hundred years, and the Mill stands on the same spot as the medieval mill that is mentioned in the Doomsday Book. Since 1921, it has been in the Mettam family who have been millers for many generations and whose family tree has been traced back to 1635. In 1993, it was lovingly restored by them and now Kate's and Ellen's husbands manage the mill while they and their four daughters run the tea shop which is housed in the Old Millwright's workshop. The entrance has a wonderful view of the water wheel and mill race and the tea shop itself looks directly over the River Maun.

This is a really delightful spot and visitors have the chance to learn a little about what life was like for a working miller in the 18th century at the same time as enjoying a really special afternoon tea in the old-fashioned style. All the cakes are baked on the premises with flour that is ground and sold in the mill. Tuck into chocolate fudge or date and walnut or go for the Ollerton Mill Cream Tea which is perfect, with three dainty fruit or plain scones served with jam and cream. *Teas served:* House Blend, Earl Grey, Assam, Darjeeling, Lady Grey. *Fruit and herbal infusions are also available.*

PASTURE FARM & VICTORIAN CARRIAGES

Owners: Helen and Mark Evans

**Pasture Farm, Main Street
Kirton, Newark
Nottinghamshire NG22 9LP
Tel: 01623 836291**

Directions
Kirton is 3½ miles from the A1 and the A614, mid-way between Ollerton and Tuxford on the A6075 Mansfield to Lincoln road. Pasture Farm is in the centre of the village, 75 yards from the church, almost opposite the Fox pub.

Opening times
Open April–September inclusive. Monday, closed. Tuesday–Sunday, 11 am–5 pm. October–March, only open Saturday and Sunday. Closed January and February.

Local Interest:
Pasture Farm has a Working Horse Drawn Carriage Driving Centre, stables and museum. You can take lessons in carriage driving, or travel by coach and four along the ancient Great North Road and quiet country by-ways, visiting friendly country inns along the way.

Pasture Farm, a traditional Nottinghamshire farmhouse, dates back to about 1800 and has retained a great deal of its original character. With its original exposed oak beamed ceiling, spacious rooms, hall ways, tall chimneys and delightful grounds, it is the perfect location in which to recreate the traditional teas of the last century.

Home cooking and value for money are the key words at Pasture Farm and everything is freshly prepared in the farmhouse kitchen. In November 1996, the excellent quality of the lunches, Cream Teas and Afternoon Teas won the Nottinghamshire County Council Tourism Award for Best Nottinghamshire Tea, sponsored by The Tea Council.

The Victorian atmosphere of Pasture Farm is heightened by the wonderful array of carriages in the museum. And there are harnesses, whips, other working carriage memorabilia, liveried coachmen, a groom, the horses he cares for and sometimes a farrier. If you would like to enjoy a ride that captures the spirit of the past, you can dress up in Victorian period costumes and be carried away in the original Victorian Landau or ride on the roof of a road coach drawn by Mark's team of four chestnut Gelderland horses before returning to the farm for a traditional tea. *Teas served:* Fine Assam, Darjeeling, Earl Grey, House Blend and other speciality teas.

ANNIE'S TEA ROOMS

Owner: Jean Ann Rowlands

**79 High Street, Wallingford
Oxfordshire OX10 0BX
Tel: 01491 836308**

Directions
Wallingford is situated at the junction of the A329, Reading to Oxford road, and the A4130, Henley to Wantage road. Annie's is in the High Street, just along from the crossroads with St Martin's Street and Castle Street.

Opening times
Open all year except Bank Holidays.
Monday, Tuesday, Thursday–Saturday,
10 am–5 pm (5.30 pm in July,
August and September).
Sunday (open only in July, August
and September), 2.30–5.30 pm.
Wednesday, closed.

Local Interest:
The castle grounds are excellent for walks and hold concerts on summer Sundays. There is a regatta in May, a carnival in June and a Victorian celebration in December when the entire town participates in entertainments and markets.

Wallingford's history goes back to the granting of its charter in 1155 and it has links with a number of interesting personalities from the past, including Oliver Cromwell. The ruins of the largest castle in England stand round the corner from Annie's and stones from here were included in the building of Windsor Castle.

Right in the centre of town, in a Grade II listed building that is over 300 years old, Jean Ann Rowlands gives a very warm welcome to visitors from all over the world who come to taste her wonderful home-baked cakes, scones, teacakes, pies and jams. Jean's speciality is her own original cinnamon-flavoured Wallingford Muffin which has a warm soft apple mixture in the middle that oozes out when you open it up.

The pretty pink and burgundy room is a relaxing setting to enjoy your tea. The walls are decorated with old paintings and views of Wallingford and paintings by local customers are displayed for sale. On fine days, a small, walled cottage garden at the back allows alfresco teas after you have explored the ancient highways and byways of the town. *Teas served:* Indian, Earl Grey, Ceylon, Darjeeling, Traditional English Blend, Assam, Lapsang Souchong. *Fruit flavoured teas and herbal infusions are also offered.*

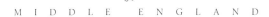

HUFFKINS

Owners: Mr and Mrs Plank

98 High Street, Burford
Oxfordshire OX18 4QF
Tel: 01993 822126

Directions
Take the A40 to Burford. The tea shop is half
way down the High Street on the left hand side.

Opening times
Open all year.
Sundays, closed.
Mondays–Fridays, 8.30 am–5.30 pm.
Saturdays, 8.30 am–6 pm.

Local Interest:
*Burford is a very attractive small town with stunningly
beautiful 15th century houses from the days of the
woollen merchants who brought wealth and importance
to the area. The local museum organises guided tours
around the town. It is also the starting point for a
circular walk along the river Windrush, to Widford
Church and across nearby farmland.*

Huffkins is so typically English and so good that visitors to this very attractive town should absolutely not miss it. Its traditional decor, with pale walls and black beams, old trestle sewing machines as tables, floral tablecloths and Victorian photographs, creates a delightful background, and the idiosyncratic and eye-catching extras – a pennyfarthing bicycle on the wall, a Victorian pram full of flowers, milkmaid's yoke and old silver teapots – add their own appealing character. In fine weather, the garden holds 20 more seats for customers who prefer to take their tea alfresco.

The menu offers all the most traditional and tempting of British fare – local cheeses and fish, wonderful tasty pickles, Welsh rarebits and sandwiches with all the favourite fillings. The Hunter's Lunch consists of baked ham, piccalilli, celery and a choice of breads, while the Cotswold Cheeses Lunch offers portions of three different cheeses, sliced apple, celery, chutney and granary bread. The selection of sweet items includes cinnamon toast, teacakes, muffins, gateaux and cream teas. And the shop counter sells teas, coffees, preserves, cakes and Belgian chocolates. *Tea served:* House Blend, Assam, Vintage Darjeeling, Earl Grey, Lapsang Souchong. *Fruit flavoured teas and herbal infusions are also available.*

RECOLLECTIONS

Owners: Chris and Hans Braendli

6 Tontine Hill
Ironbridge
Shropshire TF8 7AL
Tel: 01952 433983

Directions
From the M54, take either junction 4 or junction 6 and follow signs to Ironbridge. Recollections is situated about 100 yards from the bridge itself.

Opening times
Open May–mid-November on Saturday, Sunday, Monday, Thursday and Friday, 10.30 am–5 pm. Tuesday and Wednesday, closed. From mid-November to end April, open on Saturday and Sunday only, except during holiday periods, 10.30 am–5 pm. Telephone before visiting to check opening times.

Local Interest:
In the town and the surrounding area are the following museums - Ironbridge Gorge Museum, Toy Museum, The Museum of Iron with Darby Furnace and Quaker houses, the Jackfield Tile Museum, Blists Hill Open Air Museum with its re-creation of the town at the turn of last century, and Coalport China Museum and Tar Tunnel. There is also a wide variety of fascinating shops in the town.

Here in the heart of the birthplace of Britain's industrial revolution, Recollections is housed in a period building filled with old lights, light switches, pictures, mirrors and a collection of old tea spoons, strainers and tea tins. Its position gives it one of the best views of the Ironbridge itself, so visitors can appreciate the history of the area as well as enjoying the peaceful, relaxed, no-smoking atmosphere of the Victorian-style tearoom. A traditional theme is created by waitresses in black and white uniforms with white pinnies, and by the mix of cast iron and wood furniture set against an ointment pink and dark green decor.

For lunchtime visitors, the menu lists a good selection of home-made hot savouries, sandwiches, baguettes, omelettes with fresh herbs from the garden, toasties, soups and salads. And the Afternoon Tea menu includes hot buttered toast, teabreads, scones, home-made cakes, cream teas and a three course tea with sandwiches, scones, jam and cream and cakes. The Braendlis' awareness of the need to include low fat, healthy options on the menu recently won them a Heartbeat Award for healthy food in a healthy environment. *Teas served:* House Blend, Assam, Darjeeling, Orange Pekoe, Earl Grey, English Breakfast, Lapsang Souchong, iced tea. *Herbal infusions are also available.*

BENSON'S OF STRATFORD-UPON-AVON

Owner: Max Lawrence

**4 Bards Walk, Stratford-upon-Avon
Warwickshire CV37 6EY
Tel: 01789 261116**

Directions
Benson's is off Henley Street, two minutes walk from Shakespeare's birthplace in the town centre.

Opening times
Open all year except Sundays in winter.
Monday–Friday, 10 am–5.30 pm.
Saturday, 8.30 am–5.30 pm.
Sunday (summer only), 10 am-4.30 pm.

Local Interest:
Benson's is right in the centre of Shakespeare's town. From the shop you can easily walk to Shakespeare's birthplace, his daughter, Judith's home and Holy Trinity Church where he is buried. Also close by is Harvard House, home of the man who set up Harvard University in the USA and a place of pilgrimage for Americans.

This very light and airy conservatory-style tea shop is in a refurbished Victorian arcade that was once Osbornes Court, a row of eight little cottages converted from a Malt House between 1809 and 1821. The display of the patisseries that fills the 19th century window of the shop will tempt you inside and you will find yourself in an extremely calm and relaxing interior that is bright with the colour of the plants and flowers around the room and the original watercolours on the walls.

Max Lawrence worked in Switzerland for a while and has a flair for serving mouthwatering pastries. The mille feuille with fresh fruit is too good to miss but if you prefer something savoury with your afternoon tea, the gourmet sandwiches with all sorts of possible fillings are absolutely wonderful. Try carved ham with cream cheese and melon or Stilton with apple, or make up your own combination. A set afternoon tea will give you smoked salmon sandwiches followed by home-baked scones with jam and cream and a speciality tea served in one of the Shakespeare teapots, each of which represents a different Shakespeare play. *Teas served:* House Blend, Earl Grey, English Breakfast, Assam, Darjeeling, Ceylon, Lapsang Souchong, decaffeinated. *Herbal infusions are also offered.*

TIME FOR TEA

Owner: Helena Shaw

40 Castle Hill
Kenilworth
Warwickshire CV8 1NB
Tel: 01926 512675

Directions
Approach Kenilworth on the A452,
Birmingham to Leamington Spa route.
This becomes the B4103 which leads

directly to Kenilworth Castle. Turn left into
Castle Green and left again into Castle Hill.
Time For Tea is next to the castle and opposite
Abbey Fields.

Opening times
Open all year except Mondays. Monday, closed.
Tuesday–Sunday, 10.30 am–5 pm. 🚭

Local Interest:
*Visit Kenilworth Castle and enjoy walks in Abbey Fields
around the ruins of the Abbey and on a variety of footpaths
that start near the tea shop. The streets of the town are also
very interesting and have quaint old shops.*

Helena Shaw actually made up her mind to open her own tea shop while sitting round a table with various friends in a Darjeeling Guest House. She had been toying with the idea for some time and the situation and the encouragement of the others pushed her into vowing to do it as soon as she got back to England. Now, she is very firmly established in this lovely Grade II listed building in one of Kenilworth's prettiest streets, running an incredibly successful tea shop that everyone absolutely loves. It has very quickly become a regular haunt for locals who love the friendly, helpful, chatty atmosphere and a haven for tourists who have made such comments in the visitors' book as "Brilliant – the best tea shop in the world," and "Excellent. We'll be back!"

The charm of the two pine-furnished rooms is enhanced by a collection of pretty teapots and tea caddies that Helena has collected since she was 14 years old. Tuck into wonderful fig and walnut, honey and coconut, and chocolate orange cake. You cannot fail to enjoy yourself. *Teas served:* Earl Grey, Assam, Darjeeling, Ceylon, Lapsang Souchong, Traditional English, Jasmine. *Fruit flavoured teas and herbal infusions are also available.*

N O R T H   E A S T
R E G I O N A L   M A P

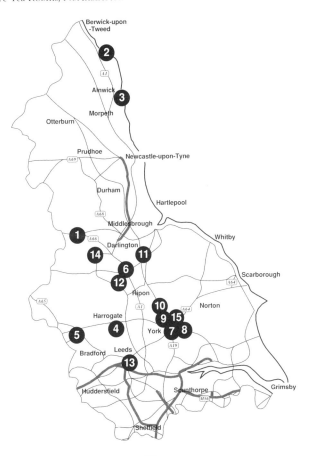

THE MARKET PLACE TEASHOP

Owner: Robert Hilton

29 Market Place, Barnard Castle
County Durham DL12 8NE
Tel: 01833 690110

Directions
The tea shop is in the centre of the cobbled Market Place.

Opening times
Open all year except two weeks at Christmas.
Monday–Saturday, 10 am–5.30 pm.
Sunday, 3–5.30 pm.

Awards
Egon Ronay recommended
Good Food Guide

Local Interest:
The town has interesting antique and craft shops in which to browse. On the outskirts, visit the Bowes Museum which has one of the finest art collections outside London, and Raby Castle, the seat of Lord Barnard. Drive to nearby High Force, the highest waterfall in England, and enjoy surrounding Teesdale countryside.

In the very heart of this attractive old market town, you will find the Market Place Teashop in an early 17th century building that long ago was a house before it became a pub and later a gentleman's outfitters selling typical country garments to local farm workers. The front of the tea shop was probably the original master's house, and servants quarters and stables were behind and alongside in Waterloo Yard. Today, the upstairs Artisan shop and picture gallery has a good selection of gifts, prints and original paintings.

The tea shop itself, which is celebrating its 26th anniversary this year, is a charming room full of character, with flagstones on the floor and an open stone fireplace. Tea is served in silver teapots by friendly waitresses in smart burgundy-striped uniforms and they will bring you whatever you choose from the tempting list of home-baked cakes that changes daily. Try the meringues filled with cream and strawberries, the strawberry tarts or the Yorkshire Curd Cheesecake. The high quality of all the food and the attractive, welcoming atmosphere make this an excellent place for lunch or afternoon tea. *Teas served:* Typhoo, Earl Grey, Ceylon, Traditional English, Assam, Darjeeling, Lapsang Souchong, China. *Fruit flavoured teas and herbal infusions are also offered.*

THE COPPER KETTLE TEA ROOMS

Owners: Rosemary Christie and David Bates

**21 Front Street, Bamburgh
Northumbria NE69 7BW
Tel: 01668 214315**

Directions
Turn off the A1 towards the coast on either the B1341 or the B1342. Both roads lead to Bamburgh and the tearoom is situated in the heart of the village.

Opening times
Monday–Friday, March, April, October, 10.30 am–5 pm; May–September, 10.30 am–5.30 pm. Saturday and Sunday, March–October, 10.30 am–5.30 pm. Closed, November–end February. Open some weekends in November and December.

Local Interest:
Visit the Norman castle and the 13th century church where you will find the grave of Grace Darling, the heroine of the rescue of survivors from a wrecked steamer. The Grace Darling Museum houses more souvenirs.

A bright display of colourful flowers outside the front door and windows welcomes you to this delightful 18th century cottage tearoom. After a tour of Bamburgh's Norman castle or a walk in the sea air, you simply must not miss afternoon tea in the old-fashioned charm of the house or cottage garden. With the exception of the bread and teacakes, everything on the tempting menu is baked on the premises and the selection is mouthwatering – gingerbread, coffee walnut cake, cherry madeira, scotch pancakes with maple syrup, and chocolate caramel shortbread, flapjacks and scones.

There is also an incredibly wide range of teas and infusions and if you want to take home more of the one you enjoyed with your tea, the gift shop offers everything from a single teabag to boxes and gift packs. And how will you be able to resist the Belgian chocolates, quality preserves, sweets and biscuits that are also displayed on the shelves?

Teas served: Assam, Ceylon, China, Darjeeling, Earl Grey, English Breakfast, Lapsang Souchong, Orange Pekoe, Rose Pouchong, decaffeinated, organic. *Fruit flavoured teas and herbal infusions are also offered.*

THE TEA COSY TEA ROOM

Owners: Sheila and Wyn Porteous

23 Northumberland Street
Alnmouth
Northumberland NE66 2RJ
Tel: 01665 830393
Fax: 01665 830393

Directions
Take the A1068 northbound from Warkworth, southbound from Alnwick. Turn right onto the B1339 at a roundabout to Alnmouth which is approximately 1 mile along this road.

Opening times
In summer, open 7 days a week, 10 am–5.30 pm.
In winter, open Tuesday–Sunday, 11 am–4 pm. Monday closed.

Local Interest:
Alnmouth itself is an interesting and picturesque village. Also, the second oldest golf course in Britain, lovely beaches, walking and fishing.

The aptly named Tea Cosy is a tea-room by day and a bistro by night and whatever time you choose to visit, you will always find a really warm welcome and friendly atmosphere. The shop sits very happily in a pretty double fronted 270 year old building and is full of character. The walls are decorated with fascinating old prints of old Alnmouth and local personalities, and the real focal point is the incredible old stone fireplace with cast iron oven that Wyn and Sheila discovered when they were doing some basic renovation work.

The Porteous' original idea was to run a village store here with a few tables, but the early success of the small tea-room led them to expand that side of the business and close down the store. Their menu is packed with local traditionals such as Northumbrian Stottie – a sort of round, flat bread – and Singing Hinnies – fruited flat griddle cakes served with butter and strawberry jam. And all the old favourites are there too – toasted muffins, hot buttered crumpets, buttery teacakes. A wide variety of home-made cakes are also available. If you are up in this part of the world, don't miss this lovely tea shop. *Teas served:* House Blend (specially blended to suit the local water), Assam, Darjeeling, Earl Grey, Lemon. *Fruit flavoured teas and herbal infusions are also offered.*

BETTYS CAFÉ TEA ROOMS

Manager: Nick Carroll

1 Parliament Street, Harrogate
North Yorkshire HG1 2QU
Tel: 01423 502746   Fax: 01423 565191

Directions
Bettys is located on the main route through the
centre of Harrogate from Leeds to Ripon,
opposite the War Memorial and overlooking
Montpellier Gardens.

Opening times
Open all year.
Monday–Sunday, 9 am–9 pm.

Awards
1990, 91, 92, 93 & 96 Tea Council Award of Excellence
1994 Tea Council Top Tea Place of The Year
Egon Ronay recommended

Local Interest:
Wander around Harrogate's wide selection of interesting
shops, or walk through Valley Gardens and Harlow Carr
Botanical Gardens. Three miles away in Knaresborough,
see the oldest chemist's shop in England and visit Mother
Shipton's Cave, the home of a 15th century prophet.

The Harrogate branch of Bettys was the first tearoom opened by Frederick Belmont in 1919. The young confectioner arrived from Switzerland and settled in North Yorkshire where he found the clear air very much to his liking. His natural talent for creating exceptionally good cakes and his Swiss flair for hospitality were the perfect combination to build a thriving business and very soon he opened more shops in other Yorkshire towns. Today, the company is still owned by direct descendents of Frederick's family, now half Swiss, half Yorkshire, but still no-one knows the identity of Betty!

Frederick Belmont's guiding principle was, "If we want things just right, we have to make them ourselves" and today, Bettys Bakery still makes all the cakes, pastries, chocolates, breads, rolls, fruit loaves, scones and muffins, and all dishes on the menu are freshly prepared on the premises.

Teas and coffees are specially imported and blended by Bettys sister company, Taylors of Harrogate. A café pianist plays every evening from 6 pm to 9 pm. *Teas served:* Tea Room Blend, Special Estate Darjeeling, Special Estate Tippy Assam, Earl Grey, Lapsang Souchong, Yunnan Flowery Orange Pekoe, China Gui Hua, Mountains of the Moon, Zulu, iced tea in summer. *Fruit flavoured teas and herbal infusions are also offered.*

Bettys Café Tea Rooms

Manager: Hilary Stammers

32–34 The Grove, Ilkley
West Yorkshire LS29 9EE
Tel: 01943 608029   Fax: 01943 816723

Directions
Bettys is in Ilkley town centre, backing on to the main Pay and Display car park and not far from the station and tourist information centre.

Opening times
Open all year.
Monday–Sunday, 9 am–6 pm.

Awards
1990, 91, 92 & 96 Tea Council Award of Excellence
1993 Tea Council Top Tea Place of The Year
Egon Ronay recommended

Local Interest:
Visit the Victorian Arcade, the Manor House Museum, the Kings Hall and Winter Gardens and drive or walk out of town across Ilkley Moor to see some of Yorkshire's most impressive countryside.

This is one of the four hugely successful Bettys Café Tea Rooms in Yorkshire and the special feature of this branch is the wonderful, colourful collection of over 200 teapots that are arranged on a high shelf that runs all round the tearoom. Recently refurbished, Bettys in Ilkley boasts a striking wrought iron canopy and extensive tea and coffee counter, stacked with antique tea caddies. The tearoom has some specially commissioned stained glass windows that depict some of the wild flowers found on the Yorkshire moors, and 'La Chasse', the largest marquetry picture ever made in the Spindler studio, which shows a medieval hunting scene.

This is a haven for ramblers who reach the town tired and in need of refreshment after walking for miles across the rugged, wind-swept moorland. They and other visitors can relax and enjoy the fabulous selection of pastries, breads and cakes that arrive fresh from Bettys Bakery every day. To add to the attraction, a pianist plays every Thursday and Sunday lunchtime and from 4.30–6 pm on Saturdays. *Teas served:* Tea Room Blend, Special Estate Darjeeling, Special Estate Tippy Assam, Earl Grey, Lapsang Souchong, Yunnan Flowery Orange Pekoe, China Gui Hua, Mountains of the Moon, Zulu, iced tea (a blend of Earl Grey and Ceylon) in summer. *Fruit flavoured teas and herbal infusions are also offered.*

BETTYS CAFÉ TEA ROOMS

Manager: Lindsay Judd

**188 High Street, Northallerton
North Yorkshire DL7 8LF
Tel: 01609 775154
Fax: 01609 777552**

Directions
Bettys is situated in the town centre, in the main shopping street.

Opening times
Open all year. Monday–Saturday, 9 am–5.30 pm. Sunday, 10 am–5.30 pm.

Awards
1987   Tea Council Top Tea Place of The Year
1990   Tea Council Award of Excellence
Egon Ronay recommended

Local Interest:
The town has a market every Wednesday and some interesting shops. It is a good centre for walking and is five miles from Old Motherley, one of the best walks in the area.

This is the smallest of the four branches of Bettys and it is a real treasure, tucked away in the Saxon market town of Northallerton. It is said that Roman soldiers once marched along the Great North Road that passes very close by and the town is mentioned in the Doomsday Book so there is lots of history here. It was in this delightful setting that Bettys opened the most recent addition to their chain of fantastic Yorkshire tea shops. The company is still owned by the family of the founder, Frederick Belmont, and teas and coffees are specially blended for the shops by the sister company, Taylors of Harrogate.

The sunny golden room here in Northallerton is small and intimate and decorated with Art Deco mirrors and antique teapots. As you step inside the red brick Georgian building, your attention will be caught by the selection of wonderful cakes and pastries that fill the counter. How does one ever decide what to eat? There are just so many delicious things to try. More than one visit is recommended in order to work your way through at least some of the selection. *Teas served:* Tea Room Blend, Special Estate Darjeeling, Special Estate Tippy Assam, Earl Grey, Lapsang Souchong, Yunnan Flowery Orange Pekoe, China Gui Hua, Mountains of the Moon, Zulu. *Fruit flavoured teas and herbal infusions are also offered.*

BETTYS CAFÉ TEA ROOMS

Manager: Sally Carter

6–8 St Helen's Square, York
North Yorkshire YO1 2QP
Tel: 01904 659142
Fax: 01904 627050

Directions
Bettys is located in the city centre, just round the corner from York Minster.

Opening times
Open all year.
Monday–Sunday, 9 am–9 pm.

Awards
Egon Ronay recommended
1997 Tea Council Award of Excellence

Local Interest:
From Bettys you can walk to the Minster, The Treasurer's House, Merchant Taylors' Hall, Yorkshire Museum and Museum Gardens, St Mary's Abbey, the Railway War Memorial, Waxworks, open air market and lots more.

This 'continental style' tearoom is set in the heart of York, and from the huge picture windows that dominate the ground floor tearoom, you can look out over the cobbled streets of this historical city. The elegant surroundings were inspired by the interior of the luxury liner, the Queen Mary. Frederick Belmont, Bettys' founder, travelled on the maiden voyage of this ocean liner in 1936, during which time he dreamt up the plans for a new flagship café in York. The liner's interior decorators were commissioned to design the new tearoom, recreating the magnificent panelling, pillars and mirrors that had adorned the Queen Mary. Many of the original 1930s features have recently been refurbished and the Belmont Room, on the first floor, has reopened after many years for group bookings and private parties.

The cakes and pastries are still made daily by hand at Bettys Craft Bakery, just as they were back in the 1930s. Today, an added attraction is the Cafe Pianist who plays every evening from 6 pm to 9 pm. *Teas served:* Tea Room Blend, Special Estate Darjeeling, Special Estate Tippy Assam, Earl Grey, Lapsang Souchong, Yunnan Flowery Orange Pekoe, China Gui Hua, Mountains of the Moon, Zulu. *Fruit flavoured teas and herbal infusions are also available.*

BULLIVANT OF YORK

Owner: Christine Bullivant

**15 Blake Street
York YO1 2QJ
Tel: 01904 671311**

Directions

From York Minster, walk along Duncombe Place to the cross roads. Turn left into Blake Street and the tea shop is about 150 yards along.

Opening times

Monday–Saturday inclusive, 9.30 am–5 pm, November–Easter. Monday, Tuesday, Wednesday, 9.30 am–6 pm, Easter–end October. Thursday, Friday, Saturday, 9.30 am–8 pm, Easter–end October. Open on Sundays. Please telephone for details.

Local Interest:

The tea shop is near all of York's main attractions - the Minster, St Mary's Abbey, York Castle, Yorkshire Museum and Museum Gardens.

Christine Bullivant's main concern is that her customers should feel pampered and relaxed in her charming, intimate tearoom and she is almost always on duty to welcome you. Her smiling and efficient staff will do their very best to make your visit a memorable one. The pretty pink decor, the pink Lloyd Loom chairs and the tables dressed in the Victorian breakfast table style make it a very special place to stop at any time of the day. A peaceful courtyard at the rear provides more seating in good weather and here you can sit surrounded by tubs full of flowers and climbing plants. Table reservations can be made.

Bullivant's menu offers an incredible range of sandwiches, club sandwiches, luncheons of wonderful cheeses, pies, pâtés, savoury pancakes and roast meats, and at tea-time all the traditional favourites are on offer – cinnamon toast, Cream Teas with delicious home-made scones with Cornish clotted cream and home-made preserves, toasted teacakes, hot buttered crumpets and a really special rich dark fruit cake that is served with Wensleydale cheese.

The shop also has an enormous range of superb Collectors' Teapots and if you are interested, Christine's helpful staff will bring items of interest to your table so that you can choose in comfort what to buy to take home with you. *Teas served include:* Select Blend, Traditional English, Earl Grey, Ceylon, Lapsang Souchong, Rose Pouchong, China, Lemon. *Fruit flavoured teas and herbal infusions are also available.*

CLARK'S OF EASINGWOLD

Owners: Judy and Gerald Clark

195 Long Street
Easingwold
York YO6 3JB
Tel: 01347 821285

Directions
Easingwold is situated equidistant between York and Thirsk and is by-passed by the A19.

Clark's is the first building on the left as you turn into the main street from the York direction. Parking is at the rear or on the road outside.

Opening times
Open all year.
Monday–Saturday, 8.30 am–4 pm (in winter), or 5 pm (in summer).

Local Interest:
Now that Easingwold has been by-passed by the A19, it is a pleasant small town in which to browse on the way to the North Yorkshire Moors or Herriot Country.

Clark's was established in 1928 by Judy Clark's grandmother-in-law who served tea and home-made scones to local cyclists from the kitchen window. She developed this promising business into a bakery, and built a wooden hut in the garden to serve as a café. This was used for many years until it was eventually demolished and replaced by the present café that was set up within the bakery shop in 1995. Now that the by-pass has eased the pressure of traffic on Easingwold, this is an extremely pleasant place to shop and browse.

Both Judy and Gerald are narrow boat enthusiasts and so have decorated the café with all sorts of canal wares to create an attractive interior – plates, pictures, posters and tea towels are displayed on shelves and on the trellis, and there is an old milk churn decorated in the style of narrow boat Buckby Ware. In good weather, there are chairs and tables in the pretty garden at the back.

The menu offers sandwiches, pies, pasties, ploughmans, soup, salads, and omelettes. Tea-time brings teacakes, scones with jam and cream, cakes and pastries, and a set tea with a selection of savouries and sandwiches, scones and cakes. Everything is made on the premises and there is a wide choice of confectionery for sale in the bakery shop. *Teas served:* Yorkshire Blend, Earl Grey.

CLARK'S TEAROOMS

Owners: Judy and Gerald Clark

Market Place, Easingwold
Yorkshire YO6 3AG
Tel: 01347 823143

Directions
Easingwold, now by-passed by A19, is 13 miles north of York and ten miles south of Thirsk.

Clark's Tearooms is situated in the market square.

Opening times
Open all year except Sundays.
Monday, Tuesday, Wednesday, 10 am–5 pm.
Thursday and Saturday, 9.30 am–5 pm.
Friday, 9 am–5 pm.
Sunday, closed.

Local Interest:
Easingwold is in the Vale of York and close to the North Yorkshire Moors and so is a good centre for walking and cycling.

All the breads, pastries and cakes served and sold at Clark's Tearooms are made at the shop's bakery that was set up 70 years ago and now houses Judy and Gerald's other tearoom and bakery shop about three quarters of a mile away on the edge of town. This main branch of the business here in the central Market Place is in the perfect location for shoppers and tourists, for either lunch or a refreshing pot of tea and one of the wonderful home-made cakes. The pretty pink and green shop is divided into three rooms with a smokers' parlour at the back. Local artists display their paintings on the walls, and traditional dark furniture is set off by rose-printed curtains and tablecloths.

The menu includes sandwiches, home-baked savouries, breads and cakes, and local specialities such as Wensleydale cheese, Yorkshire fruit cake, Yorkshire curd tarts, and delicious fruit pies with cream. If you would like to buy some of these to take home, the Clarks have a bakery shop on the other side of the street which sells their breads, pastries and cakes. *Teas served:* House Blend, Darjeeling, Earl Grey. *Fruit flavoured teas and herbal infusions are also offered.*

CRATHORNE HALL HOTEL

General Manager: Mark Booth

**Crathorne Hall Hotel
Crathorne, Near Yarm
North Yorkshire TS15 0AR
Tel: 01642 700398**

Directions
Crathorne Hall is close to the A19 trunk road at Crathorne Village. From the south, take the slip road marked for A67 Yarm, Teeside Airport and Kirklevington. From the north, take slip road A67 to Crathorne Village.

Opening times
Open all year. 7 am–10.30 pm every day.

Awards
1997 The Tea Council Award of Excellence

Local Interest:
There are castles (Richmond, Barnard, Middleham, Pickering), museums (Bowes, Beamish, The Jorvik Viking Museum), stately homes (Castle Howard, Ormesby Hall, Fairfax House), ruins (Rivaulx, Easby, Kirkham, Byland), Yorkshire Steam railway, racing (Ripon, Thirsk, York), Flamingo Land Zoo and Park, and beautiful Yorkshire coastline and beaches.

Crathorne Hall is one of Britain's finest Edwardian houses, built in 1906 and set in 15 acres of fine wooded grounds between the Yorkshire Dales and the North Yorkshire Moors. Many of the original features remain intact, including large stone fireplaces, ornate ceilings, wooden panelling and generous bay windows. The Drawing Room, the venue for Yorkshire Cream Teas and Afternoon Tea, boasts some very fine paintings, windows that open on to the spacious lawns where croquet is played in summer, and offers the welcome of roaring log fires in winter. The hotel's gastronomic team has created an impressive range of menus for different occasions, including the Grandma Pomfret selection of traditional desserts, which comes from recipes handed down from generation to generation. The hotel also runs Speciality Break weekends – three on offer are wine appreciation, petits fours skills, and murder mystery weekends! But if it's just tea you want, you will not be disappointed. This is a wonderful, elegant, relaxing location and really is perfect for stylish teas. *Teas served:* Breakfast Blend, China, Darjeeling, Indian, Earl Grey. *Various fruit flavoured teas and herbal infusions are also available.*

THE MAD HATTER TEA SHOP

Owners: Andrew Atkinson and
Stirling Jebb

**Market Place, Masham
Near Ripon, North Yorkshire
HG4 4EA
Tel: 01765 689129**

Directions
Masham is 20 miles north of Harrogate on the
A61 between Glasshouses and Jervaulx and

8 miles west of the A1 of the B6267. The tea
shop is in the heart of the town in the market
square.

Opening times
Open all year except Thursday. Monday,
Tuesday, Wednesday, Friday, Saturday, 10 am–
5 pm. Sunday, 11 am–5 pm. Thursday, closed.

Local Interest:
*Nestling at the foot of the Yorkshire Dales. Masham offers
year-round attractions for keen walkers and afternoon
strollers. There are two local breweries (visitors welcome),
and a busy market in the Old Market Square every
Wednesday and Saturday.*

The Mad Hatter occupies a 200 year old Grade II listed building in the centre of Masham. Since taking over the business in February 1997, Andrew and Stirling have expanded the business by opening up the first floor room that has a view over the Old Market Square, and have created a comfortable lounge with sofa and armchairs in which to settle back and enjoy a perfect "cuppa". They have also restored many of the original features of the building and, "given Andrew's ability at icing cakes, we had imagined that plastering walls would not prove too difficult, but alas, there is a difference and we had to call in a plasterer (he told us, "it's as simple as icing a cake!!"")".

The look throughout the shop is traditional, with each table covered with hand-embroidered tablecloths.

The menu includes plenty of healthy options – salads, jacket potatoes with unusual fillings such as prawn and avocado, vegetarian cheddar, apple and onion, and open sandwiches which pose a challenge even for the biggest appetites – and the ever-changing range of cakes includes favourites such as ginger and lemon, apricot and amaretto, and American baked cheesecake. *Teas served:* Assam, Ceylon, Darjeeling, China, Earl Grey, English Breakfast, Formosa Lapsang Souchong, Yorkshire. *Fruit flavoured teas and herbal infusions are also available.*

OULTON HALL HOTEL

Owner: De Vere Hotels
Manager: Rhodri Mitchell

**Rothwell Lane
Oulton, Leeds
Yorkshire LS26 8HN
Tel: 01132 821000
Fax: 01132 828066**

Directions
Take junction 42 off the M1 or junction 30 off the M62. Follow signs for Rothwell.

Opening times
Open all year.
Tea is served in the Drawing Room which is open Monday–Sunday, 10 am–6 pm.

Local Interest:
The hotel's Leisure Club offers a swimming pool, a golf course, a gym, squash courts, sauna and steam room. Also visit York, the Yorkshire Dales and the National Photographic Museum in Bradford.

Oulton Hall stands on the high ground above the Yorkshire village of Oulton. It was originally a simple farmhouse but was rebuilt as an elegant hall in the early 19th century. After a major fire in 1850, the house was again remodelled and extended, making it truly a mansion, complete with Great Hall and Gallery. During this century, it gradually fell into disrepair and was threatened with demolition until first Leeds City Council bought it and then De Vere Hotels rescued it. The wonderfully restored Hall stands in the most beautiful parkland, and around the house are 19th century gardens that are Grade II listed in the English Register of Historic Gardens.

This elegant setting creates a sense of stepping back in time to the days when afternoon tea was the highlight of many people's day. Tea at Oulton Hall, an AA 5 star hotel, is served in the Drawing Room where the menu offers a selection of mouthwatering sandwiches (chilled prawns with Marie Rose sauce, turkey breast with cranberry sauce and crisp lettuce), delicious cakes, including a fruit cake that is served with Wensleydale cheese, and scones with clotted cream and strawberry jam. The very friendly, welcoming atmosphere will ensure that you really feel at home. *Teas served:* House Blend, Ceylon, Darjeeling, Assam, Earl Grey, Lapsang Souchong and more. *Camomile infusion is also available.*

THE PRIEST'S HOUSE

Owners: Robert Hodgson and
Jo Parkinson

**Barden, Near Skipton
North Yorkshire BD23 6AS
Tel: 01756 720616**

Directions
From Leeds, take the A65 to Addingham.
Follow directions to Bolton Abbey. Take the
B6160 to Burnsall. Barden is between Bolton
Abbey and Burnsall, approximately 3 miles
from Bolton Abbey. You will see the ruins of
Barden Tower on the right. The gateway is
signposted.

Opening times
Open mid-March–end October,
10.30 am–5.30 pm.
Closed Thursday and Friday.

Local Interest:
*Bolton Abbey is 3 miles away. Lovely riverside and
moorland walks. Strid Wood (Special Site of Scientific
Interest SSSI) is a mile away.*

The tearooms lie in the heart of the beautiful Yorkshire Dales, located in a 15th century building next to the ruins of Barden Tower. Since establishing the business here in 1991, Robert and Jo have built up a regular trade with summer visitors to the area.

You can take tea either outside over-looking the ruins or inside in the Oak room – so called because of its oak beamed ceiling and magnificent oak dressers which house a fine collection of antique Willow Pattern meat platters (echoed in the crockery used in the tearoom). Many people comment on the wonderfully relaxed atmosphere of the Oak Room with its historic features and gentle period background music.

Light refreshments are served throughout the day. Afternoon Tea is always popular, both in summer when sultana and lemon scones with jam and cream are a particular favourite, and in winter months when customers prefer toasted crumpets or fruit loaf by the log fire.

The water from the shop's moorland spring makes fantastic tea and some customers even bring bottles to fill so that they can take some away to enjoy at home. *Teas served:* Traditional Blend, Assam, Darjeeling, Earl Grey, Lapsang Souchong, Sri Lanka Golden. *Herbal infusions are also available.*

TAYLORS IN STONEGATE

Manager: Janet Parker

46 Stonegate, York
North Yorkshire YO1 2AS
Tel: 01904 622865
Fax: 01904 640348

Directions
Taylors is very close to York Minster in Petergate.

Opening times
Open all year.
Monday–Sunday, 9 am–5.30 pm.

Awards
1991, 92 & 93   Tea Council Award of Excellence
Egon Ronay recommended

Local Interest:
Within walking distance of the tearoom are York Minster, The Treasurer's House, the Merchant Taylors' Hall, St Mary's Abbey, Yorkshire Museum and Museum Gardens, Waxworks, York Castle and Museum, Cliffords Tower, Coppergate Shopping Centre and so much more.

It is evident from the 18th century name of a nearby snickleway, 'Coffee Yard', that Stonegate has had associations with coffee since long before Taylors set up in business as tea and coffee merchants in 1886. Two brothers, Charles and Llewellyn Taylor, established the family business in what is now a Grade II listed building in the heart of medieval York. Over the years, the brothers acquired a discerning clientele and even supplied the coffee for King Edward VII's coronation. Today, it is the very epitome of a perfect English tearoom.

In 1962, Taylors became part of the Bettys family business and is one of five world-famous tearooms with an outstanding selection of teas and coffees, chocolates, breads, cakes and Yorkshire specialities such as Fat Rascals, Spiced Yorkshire Teacakes and Yorkshire Curd Tart.

Once you have tried and become addicted to the excellent foods and teas, you can have a regular supply sent by post by telephoning Harrogate 01423 886055. *Teas served:* Stonegate Tearoom Blend, Choice Assam, Special Estate Tippy Assam, Fine Darjeeling BOP, Vintage Darjeeling, Fine Ceylon BOP, Ceylon Orange Pekoe, Earl Grey, Keemun, Lapsang Souchong, Mountains of the Moon, China Gui Hua, Japanese Cherry, Zulu. *Fruit flavoured teas and herbal infusions are also offered.*

N O R T H   W E S T
R E G I O N A L   M A P

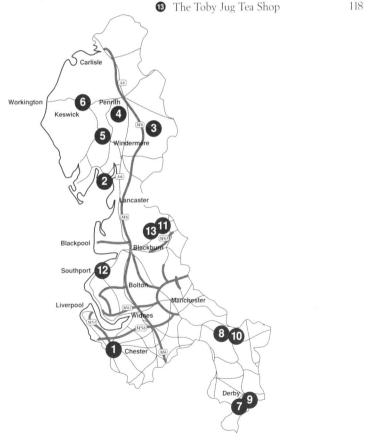

KATIES TEA ROOMS

Manager: Katie O'Brien

Watergate Street
Chester CH1 2LA
Tel: 01244 400322
Fax: 01244 400323

Directions
Watergate Street runs from The Cross to the racecourse and Katies is 100 yards along on the right.

Opening times
Open all year except Christmas Day, Boxing Day and New Year's Day.
In winter, Monday, 9.30 am–6 pm.
Tuesday–Saturday, 8 am–6 pm.
Sunday, 10 am–5 pm.
In summer, open until 9 pm.

Local Interest:
Chester is an ancient Roman town and has good shops, old city walls, interesting architectural features and very attractive surrounding countryside.

Katies is thought to be Britain's largest tearoom, with seating for more than 200 guests. It is housed in two of Chester's oldest brick and timber-framed stone buildings dating back to the early 14th century. The remains of a large medieval house, built for a wealthy merchant, consist of a line of cellars and undercrofts, merchant's hall that was the living area for the family, storage rooms and private chamber. The restored space creates an amazing setting for this really top quality restaurant and tearooms where staff are traditionally dressed in black and white and the quality service is friendly and efficient. The menu, which is on sale as a souvenir, is beautifully styled and illustrated with reproduction prints of Watergate Street in the 1830s and of the original layout of the house. Its contents offer an excellent range of hot and cold lunchtime treats, children's specials, a good range of soft drinks and wines, and an appetising variety of tea-time sandwiches, traditionals (hot buttered crumpets, cinnamon toast, Scottish pancakes, scones with clotted cream) and cakes (carrot, banana bread, shortbreads and fresh cream cakes) and a full afternoon tea. *Teas served:* Chester Blend, Assam, Darjeeling, Earl Grey, Lapsang Souchong, Jasmine, Keemun, Rose Petal. *Fruit flavoured teas and herbal infusions are also available.*

HAZELMERE CAFE & BAKERY

Owners: Dorothy and Ian Stubley

1 Yewbarrow Terrace
Grange over Sands
Cumbria LA11 6ED
Tel: 015395 32972
Fax: 015395 32972

Directions
When coming into Grange over Sands on the B5277, you will pass Grange station on the left. Shortly after this, there is a mini-roundabout. Take the first exit and the Cafe is about 25 yards along, on the right.

Opening times
Open all year.
10 am–4.30 pm in winter,
9.30 am–5.30 pm in summer.

Local Interest:
The Hazelmere overlooks Grange's famous ornamental gardens. The bay is a perfect place for walks on the sand and a short ride by car will take you up into the Lake District.

Grange over Sands is one of those towns that just would not be complete without a high-class tea shop, and the Hazelmere, set in a parade of Victorian shops fronted by a beautiful ornate glass and cast iron verandah provides the perfect venue for tea, and also manages to recapture the spirit of traditional tea-time. Dorothy and Ian Stubley specialise in home-made quality food using only the best ingredients, including free-range eggs and fresh cream. They make everything on the premises and like to include a mixture of local specialities as well as their own original recipes.

Since the Stubleys also have their own bakery and bakery shop and were winners of Bake '93 for the North West region, you can be absolutely sure that you will not be disappointed by the selection of real treats – Cumberland rum nicky, Yorkshire curd tart, date and walnut fudge tart, and sandwiches filled with Cheddar cheese and home-made apricot chutney or succulent roasted beef with whole grain honey mustard. Light meals are also available. *Teas served*: House Blend (Brunswick Estate B.O.P. Ceylon), Earl Grey, Lapsang Souchong, 4 Single Estate Ceylon, Single Estate Indonesian, 3 China, Darjeeling. *Fruit flavoured teas and herbal infusions are also available.*

NEW VILLAGE TEA ROOMS

Owner: Christine Evans

**Orton, Penrith
Cumbria CA10 3RH
Tel: 015396 24886**

Directions
Leave the M6 at junction 38 and take the Appleby road. In Orton, take the Shap road in front of the George Hotel. The tearooms are straight ahead, opposite the stores and Post Office, where the road turns left and leaves the village.

Opening times
Open all year.
July–August, 10 am–6 pm. April, May, June, September, October, 10 am–5 pm.
November, March, 10.30 am–4.30 pm.

Local Interest:
Orton is an interesting village with buildings dating back to the 17th and 18th centuries. It is an ideal centre for visits to the Lake District, the Yorkshire Dales, the North Pennines, the Border Country and Morecambe Bay. The Wainwright 'Coast to Coast' walk (from St Bees to Robin Hood's Bay) touches the village.

The New Village Tea Rooms are housed in an 18th century building which has had a varied history and was most recently a cottage. The downstairs tearoom was once the cottage living room and the kitchen is open to the friendly area where customers now sit to enjoy their tea. This means that they can chat to the staff while their food is being prepared and feel really at home.

On hot summer days, the tearooms remain cool and comfortable but sunlovers can bask outside in the pretty cottage garden. In winter, an open coal fire keeps visitors warm and cosy and creates a haven for walkers. Californian 'Coast to Coast' walkers who visited when walking west to east in 1992 and again when walking east to west in 1994, said that the sticky toffee pudding was the best in the country and took the recipe home, vowing to keep it a secret forever.

All the food is prepared on the premises using traditional methods and locally produced quality ingredients. The menu offers a wide range of home-made cakes, tempting desserts, sandwiches and hot lunch dishes in a totally smoke-free environment. *Teas served:* Earl Grey, Ceylon, Darjeeling, Assam, Lapsang Souchong, PG Tips. *Fruit flavoured teas and herbal infusions are also offered.*

SHARROW BAY COUNTRY HOUSE HOTEL

Owners: Francis Coulson and Brian Sack

Lake Ullswater, Howtown
Cumbria CA10 2LZ
Tel: 017684 86301   Fax: 017684 86349

Directions
Leave the M6 at Junction 40 and travel west on the A66 to Keswick and Ullswater. At the roundabout, take the 1st exit on to the A592 to Ullswater. At the T-junction, turn left into Pooley Bridge. Travel through the village and take the right fork at the church, signposted to Howtown. At the crossroads, turn right to Howtown and follow Lake Road for 2 miles.

Opening times – BOOKING ESSENTIAL
Open from the end of February–the end of November. Monday–Sunday, 7.30 am–10.30 pm.

Awards
1997 Tea Council Award of Excellence

Local Interest:
Sharrow Bay Hotel is positioned right on the edge of Lake Ullswater and there are spectacular walks in all directions. Two old steamers carry passengers up and down the lake and stop at Pooley Bridge and Howtown, both quite close to the hotel.

When Francis Coulson opened Sharrow Bay Country House Hotel in 1949, food was rationed, petrol was rationed, there was no motorway, and the Lake District wasn't considered to be very fashionable. But, Francis very quickly gained a reputation for wonderful afternoon teas with cakes and scones that he made to recipes taught him by his mother. Today, the reputation has grown, not just for afternoon tea but for the wonderful accommodation, gracious and caring staff, a calm and peaceful ambience, the huge traditional English breakfasts and amazing dinners.

Afternoon Tea remains the real speciality of the house. Just as in the early days, everything is baked on the premises and the superb cakes include Grasmere gingerbread, Genoese cream sponges, dainty tartlets, lemon cake that is absolutely soaked with sugary juice, meringues and various other cakes.

Tea is served in two lounges and the conservatory, with Minton china on elegant silver trays. If you choose the drawing room, the view across Lake Ullswater is probably one of the finest in England. BOOKING IS ESSENTIAL FOR TEA. *Teas served:* English Breakfast, Darjeeling, Ceylon, Indian, Earl Grey, Lapsang Souchong, China. *Fruit flavoured teas and herbal infusions are also available.*

SHEILA'S COTTAGE

Owners: Janice and Stewart Greaves

The Slack, Ambleside
Cumbria LA22 9DQ
Tel: 015394 33079
Fax: 015394 34488

Directions

Turn under an archway off the Market Place
and walk down a narrow lane to the tea shop.

Opening times

**Open February–end December. Closed January.
Monday, 11 am–5 pm. Tuesday–Saturday,
11 am–9.30 pm. Sunday (February, March,
April and November, December), 11 am–5 pm.**

Awards

1990   Tea Council Award of Excellence
Egon Ronay recommended

Local Interest:

*Ambleside is a typical lakeland town at the head
of Lake Windermere, the largest of the lakes. Visit Bridge
House, thought to be the 17th century summer house of a
mansion that has long since disappeared, and Adrian
Sankey's glass blowing workshop. Steamers leave from
Waterhead for Lakeside and Bowness.*

In the 1950s, Stewart and Janice Greaves owned a holiday cottage in the Ambleside area which was called Sheila's Cottage, after Stewart's mother, and in which they spent many happy times. So when they bought an empty cottage in the town in the 60s they used the same name and have been in business there for 33 very successful years. The cottage is a typical 250 year old lakeland, slate-roofed building which was used in Victorian days as shelter for coachmen whose passengers stayed in the smarter inns in the main square. Today, the interior of the quaint cottage and the adjoining barn is typical lakeland cottage style, with papered walls, dark country furniture and windows decked out with flowers.

The traditional style menu includes breads and muffins made with local flour and a lakeland Afternoon Tea with Borrowdale Tea Bread (made with fruit steeped in tea), Lancashire cheese, potted trout and shrimps, fresh scones with home-made strawberry jam and tea desserts – all served on fine Swiss porcelain. A dessert not to be missed is Savarin's – a traditional French yeast cake soaked in Kirsch syrup and filled with raspberries and chantilly cream. *Teas served:* Ceylon, Darjeeling, Broken Orange Pekoe, Earl Grey, Keemun.

THE WILD STRAWBERRY

Owners: James and Margaret Wilkinson

54 Main Street
Keswick
Cumbria CA12 5JS
Tel: 017687 74399

Directions
The tea shop is situated on Keswick's Main Street, near the Post Office, just off the lower end of the market square, with good views of the Moot Hall.

Opening times
Open all year except 4 weeks from mid-January–mid-February. Monday, Tuesday, Thursday, Friday, Saturday, 10 am–5 pm. Wednesday, 10 am–5 pm in season. Sunday, 11 am–5 pm.

Local Interest:
As the largest town in the Lake District National Park, Keswick is an ideal centre for enjoying the area. Also visit the Cumberland Pencil Museum, the Motor Museum, local potters' workshops, 18th century Moot Hall, traders' market every Saturday in the Market Square, Victorian Fair in December and jazz festival in May.

The friendly, cheery tearoom is housed in a 17th century cottage that was once a Cumberland pencil-maker's workshop, and still has its oak beams and flagged floor made from local green slate. The floor of the upstairs room is covered with a carpet made from the wool of Herdwick sheep made famous by Beatrix Potter, and the strawberry theme of the cottage name is continued in the design of the bone china tableware which is specially made for the tearoom. The interior of the cottage is enhanced by photos and personally embroidered pictures, giving a lovely homely feel.

James and Margaret Wilkinson have 35 years of experience in the catering trade and both play an active part in the tearoom, which is very popular with locals and tourists alike. Freshly-baked home-made fayre – and especially the delicious scones and sticky toffee pudding – make choosing a really difficult pleasure! The tearoom's speciality is a fatless and sugar-free fruit tea bread. *Teas served:* House Blend, Assam, Darjeeling, Earl Grey, Ceylon. *Various herbal infusions are also available.*

BROOK FARM TEA ROOMS

Owners: Sue and Dave Goodwin

Brook Farm, Repton
Derbyshire DE65 6FW
Tel: 01283 702215

Directions
From the A38, take the turning to Willington. In Willington, follow signs to Repton. Turn left at the monument island and the tearoom is 150 yards away on the left and well signposted from the road.

Opening times
Open in early April.
Please telephone to confirm.

Award
Egon Ronay recommended

Local Interest:
The main part of Repton village was designated a conservation area in 1969 and there are 40 listed buildings. Repton is famous for the Crypt, the final resting place of the Mercian kings who lived here from the 7th-9th centuries, and Repton School, established in 1557. Surrounding countryside is excellent for walking, riding and cycling.

The old sandstone and brick barn that houses Brook Farm Tea Rooms has, over the years, served many functions as part of the working farm. Now, its A-framed wooden roof, white walls, wood-panelled walls and Rayburn stove create a cosy, farmhouse atmosphere where friendly, thoughtful waitresses serve you with a ready smile. The large patio windows allow visitors a view of a grassy bank that slopes gently down to the brook and of the courtyard where calves and other small farm animals are kept in winter.

Sue and Dave Goodwin are very concerned that their customers feel relaxed and comfortable while here and their garden, well away from main roads and with plenty of seating on the lawns, is a quiet and safe place for families. And, because everything is on the flat and easily accessible, it is a perfect place for visitors who find stairs difficult or are wheelchair-bound.

The food is quality home-baking that appeals to everyone, and children (and quite possibly adults too) will love the farmhouse dairy ice creams that tempt you with such flavours as lemon meringue, melon and ginger, blackberry and rum and raisin. *Teas served:* Traditional Typhoo, Earl Grey, Darjeeling, English Breakfast, Assam. *Fruit flavoured teas and herbal infusions are also offered.*

THE COTTAGE TEA ROOM

Owners: Bill and Betty Watkins

3 Fennel Street, Ashford-in-the-Water Near Bakewell, Derbyshire DE45 1QF Tel: 01629 812488

Directions
Ashford-in-the-Water lies on the A6, two miles north of Bakewell and eight miles south of Buxton Spa. The tearoom is just above the ford by the ancient sheepwash bridge.

Opening times
Open all year except Tuesdays and Fridays, one week in mid-September, Christmas Day, Boxing Day and New Year's Day. Monday, Wednesday, Thursday, 2.30–5 pm. Tuesday and Friday, closed. Saturday and Sunday, 10.30 am–12 noon, 2.30–5 pm.

Award
Egon Ronay recommended

Local Interest:
Ashford-in-the-Water, once part of the Duke of Devonshire's Chatsworth Estate, is considered to be the jewel of The Peak District National Park. Five bridges span the River Wye (famous amongst anglers). The Norman church contains examples of the local coloured marble and there is a carefully restored 14th century tithe barn.

You take a step back in time when you find the charming Cottage Tea Room in this unspoilt village on the old Drovers Road from Inverness to London. Here, journeymen and visitors have paused for refreshment for many a day, long before the Peak District became the nation's first National Park.

The unchanging quality is the treasured feature of Betty and Bill Watkins' tearoom where customers are served at lace-covered tables with freshly brewed leaf tea and dainty bakery as were their grandparents in earlier decades. Open throughout the year, a friendly welcome awaits you on sun-drenched summer days and on snowy winter ones when tea by an open fire is especially tempting.

The accent is on genuine home cooking. There is a wonderful array of traditional English cakes and hand-kneaded breads, and a variety of feather-light scones is baked daily. The warm cheesy herb scones are a great favourite on winter days. Six set meals are served and you can choose anything from a simple pot of tea and a slice of cake to the full afternoon tea. *Teas served:* In addition to the specially blended House tea, an extensive selection of leaf teas is available, including 6 China, 5 Ceylon, 3 Indian, Kenya, Formosa Oolong, Russian Caravan, Earl Grey and English Breakfast. *A range of herbal infusions is also provided.*

Mrs KEMPS

Manager: Loreen Black

Elvaston Castle
Elvaston Country Park, Borrowash
Derby DE72 3EP
Tel: 01332 755796
Fax: 01332 755796

Directions
Follow brown tourist signs to Elvaston Country

Park from the A52 or A6. Elvaston Castle lies 5 miles south east of Derby and 10 miles east of Nottingham on the B5010.

Opening times
Open all year.
10 am–4.30 pm every day.

Local Interest:
The Country Park is set in beautiful countryside and includes wonderful mature grounds (designed by Capability Brown) with a lake, trees and formal parterre gardens. The Gothic hall adjoining the tearoom is used as a venue for medieval banquets and summer balls.

Elvaston Castle was built in 1834 in gothic style and is an ideal place for special events, business luncheons, marriages and wedding receptions, dinner dances and parties that take place in the Gothic hall, while lunches and Afternoon Teas are served in what was once the sitting room. The Grade II listed house was the historic home of the Earls of Harrington who owned it until the 1960s, and one section of the building dates back to 1633. The rest was built in the 1830s by Beau Petersham for his fiancée. There is space for 84 guests in the tearoom which has some fine period ceiling mouldings and plasterwork and is furnished in Victorian style with

linen tablecloths over wooden tables. Waitresses are dressed in traditional black and white with broderie anglaise tabards and headbands.

For lunch, guests can choose from an appetising range of salads, hot savouries and sandwiches made on wonderful breads flavoured with sun dried tomatoes, fresh basil, garlic, bell peppers, rosemary and olive oil. At tea-time, the menu includes traditionals and home-baked cakes such as carrot cake, yoghurt cake and – "an absolute must" – chocolate orange ring. *Teas served:* Assam, Darjeeling, English Breakfast, Irish Breakfast, Afternoon Blend, Earl Grey. *Fruit flavoured teas and herbal infusions are also available.*

NORTHERN TEA MERCHANTS

Owner: David Pogson

Crown House
193 Chatsworth Road, Brampton
Chesterfield, Derbyshire S40 2BA
Tel: 01246 233243
Fax: 01246 555991

Directions
Northern Tea Merchants is situated one mile from the centre of Chesterfield on the A619 (the road to Chatsworth House).

Opening times
Open all year except Bank Holidays, for a week from Christmas to New Year, and Sundays.
Monday–Friday, 9 am–5 pm.
Saturday, 9 am–4.30 pm. Sunday, closed.

Local Interest:
Chesterfield's crooked spire on the Church of St Mary and All Saints is a famous tourist attraction, and don't miss the interior of the church, the market place and conservation area with its early 16th century timber-framed inn.

The windows of Northern Tea Merchants' double-fronted store, not far from the famous crooked spire, are full of eye-catching tea and coffee equipment – scales, caddies, grinders, tea chests, tea wares, and attractive packages. The family business, dating back to 1936, specialises in tea blending and packing and the manufacture of tea bags (as well as coffee roasting, grinding and packaging), and handles enough for 100 million cups a year. Proprietor David Pogson is recognised as an authority on tea and acts as a judge in Tea Council tea-tasting competitions. His shop is an absolute treasure trove of speciality teas, coffees and equipment, and shelves are stacked high with an incredible choice of packages. This is a place of serious tea drinking where you can sample some of the unusual varieties at the tea bar before selecting your purchases from a range of 24 blends and single source teas. Visitors can also choose from a mouthwatering selection of scones, cakes and pastries to accompany their tea. *Teas served:* Golden De Luxe Classic, Silver De Luxe, Quayside Blend, Caddy Tea, Darjeeling, Assam, Ceylon, Ceylon Orange Pekoe, Keemun, Lapsang Souchong, Earl Grey, English Breakfast, Kenya, Russian Caravan, Formosa Oolong, Gunpowder, Jasmine. *Fruit flavoured teas and herbal infusions are also available.*

CAPRICE TEA SHOP

Owners: Peter and Joyce Jenkinson

6–8 Moor Lane
Clitheroe
Lancashire BB7 1BE
Tel: 01200 422034

Directions
Leave the A49 at the Clitheroe turn off. On entering the town centre, Caprice is on the left hand side in the parade of shops before the entrance to the castle.

Opening times
Open all year.
Monday, Tuesday, Thursday, Friday, Saturday, 9.30 am–4.30 pm.
Wednesday and Sunday, closed.

Local Interest:
Clitheroe has a castle with a Norman keep and a good museum, the library is housed in an interesting building dating back to 1800, and the Tourist Information Centre organises walks through the town that give you all the history.

The generous picture windows on both sides of Caprice's double-fronted façade provide ample space for several tables at which customers can enjoy lunch or tea while watching the world go by. The interior is on two levels with walls decorated in calm neutral shades and a dusky pink carpet, while black bentwood chairs and paintwork give an elegance that tones with the stylish black and gold exterior.

The inspiration for some of the dishes on Caprice's menu comes from the range of traditional cookbooks that Joyce collects and displays in the shop. So, favourite lunchtime savouries include delicious home-made soups, beef casserole with parsley dumplings, roast leg of lamb with mint sauce, and steak and kidney pudding, a selection of traditional desserts (Manchester Tart, fruit crumbles, lemon meringue pie, and banana and chocolate bread and butter pudding served with custard, cream or ice cream) and a long list of home-made cakes and pastries that include flapjacks, apple and cinnamon slice, vanilla custard bake and Cumbrian lemon cake. Or try some of the imaginative and delicious scones – choose from fruit, plain, cherry and almond, ginger, orange and lemon, cheese, or cheese with sundried tomato. Everything on the menu is cooked by Joyce on the premises and is made with local produce. *Teas served:* House Blend, Assam, Darjeeling, Ceylon, Earl Grey. *Herbal infusions are also available.*

NOSTALGIA TEAROOMS

Owner: Ann Couzens

215–217 Lord Street, Southport
Lancashire PR8 1NZ
Tel: 01704 501294

Directions
Nostalgia is opposite the Tourist Information
Centre, on the first floor of the black and white
building, above The Early Learning Centre.

Opening times
Open all year. Monday, open only in
July and August, 9.30 am–5 pm.
Tuesday–Saturday, 9.30 am–5 pm.
Sunday, 10 am–5 pm.

Local Interest:
*Southport has a steam locomotive museum, the Atkinson
Art Gallery, Warfarers Arcade with its statue of Red Rum
and Marine Lake with fun fair, boating, walks and a
miniature railway.*

Ann Couzens had already enjoyed considerable success with her first tearoom in Birkdale before opening this Southport branch in one of the town's typical Victorian arcades. Ann used to be a catering teacher in one of the local schools and several of her staff are past pupils whom she has trained individually in the traditional preparation, presentation and service of food and in customer relations. She also designed the furniture and the interior decoration herself so that the large airy room would look absolutely right. Styled on a conservatory, with bamboo chairs and a colour scheme in pale pink and green, this is an elegant and restful place to take tea, where waitresses in pretty Victorian black and white costumes look after you in the old-fashioned way.

The generous menu which is supplemented by a daily blackboard, includes modern as well as traditional cakes – the Pavlova and Choux gateau are extremely tempting. And there are ice cream sundaes with exotic names such as Mississippi Steamboat and Singapore Surprise. But, even if you settle for just a cup of tea and a flapjack, you are bound to enjoy the reassuring Englishness of the experience. *Teas served:* Yorkshire Gold Premium, English Breakfast, Earl Grey, Darjeeling, Ceylon, Assam. *Fruit flavoured teas and herbal infusions are also offered.*

THE TOBY JUG TEA SHOP

Owners: Peter and Marie Ireland

20 King Street, Whalley
Clitheroe, Lancashire
BB7 9SL
Tel: 01254 823298
Fax: 01254 823298

Directions
The Toby Jug is in the main street of Whalley Village, by the bridge over the River Calder.

Opening times
Open all year except Sundays and Mondays.
Open Tuesday–Friday, 10 am–4.30 pm, Saturday, 10.30 am–5 pm.

Local Interest:
Whalley is an attractive village with some good shops and a parish church that has some interesting Saxon crosses in the churchyard. The Cistercian Abbey is mostly in ruins but the Chapter House is still used as a retreat.

The Toby Jug Tea Shop, originally King Street Farm and now a Grade II listed building, would, in days gone by, have provided a welcome resting place for weary pilgrims on their way to the mother church in Whalley, which dates back to 1206 and today houses the beautiful 15th century choir stalls taken from the Cistercian Abbey nearby. In the churchyard are three Celtic preaching crosses. The village, in the heart of the Ribble Valley, nestles beneath Pendle Hill, where the Quaker founder, George Fox, preached in 1652, and which is closely associated with the infamous Pendle witches and their subsequent trial and hanging in Lancaster in 1612.

The Toby Jug, the Ireland's family home, offers traditional Lancashire hospitality and creates a cosy atmosphere with its oak beams and panelling plundered from the Abbey. The menu is packed with delicious lunchtime savouries and sandwich ideas, and for tea there are scones and an extensive range of tempting cakes, gateaux and fruit pies, all made on the premises and so reminiscent of days gone by. *Teas served:* Yorkshire Blend, Assam, Earl Grey, Darjeeling, English Breakfast, Lapsang Souchong, Jasmine Blossom, Orange and Lemon, decaffeinated. *Peppermint infusion is also available.*

W A L E S

R E G I O N A L   M A P

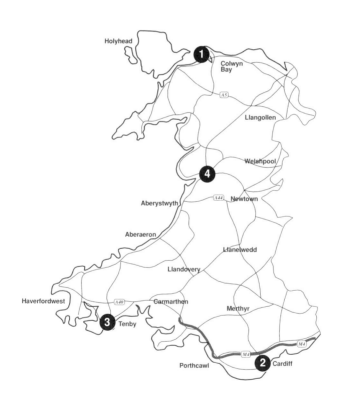

St TUDNO HOTEL

Owners: Martin and Janette Bland

Promenade, Llandudno
Gwynedd LL30 2LP
Tel: 01492 874411
Fax: 01492 860407

Directions
From the A55 take the A470 Llandudno
Link road. On reaching the Promenade,
drive towards the Great Orme headland. The
hotel is directly opposite the pier entrance and
ornamental gardens.

Opening times
Open all year, 7 am–11 pm.

Award
1996 & 97 Tea Council Award of Excellence
Egon Ronay recommended

Local Interest:
The town, with its Victorian pier, gardens and beach, is ideally located for exploring North Wales. Nearby there are castles, National Trust properties and the world famous gardens at Bodnant.

The St Tudno Hotel enjoys a reputation as one of the most luxurious seaside resort hotels in Great Britain and has won an amazing number of awards over the years. Martin and Janette Bland, with their unique flair for hotel keeping and incredibly high standards, really deserve all the accolades. The hotel interiors are wonderfully glamorous, the staff are extremely attentive and the atmosphere is one of charm and warmth and meticulous care. And an extra item of interest is the fact that Alice Liddell, immortalised by Lewis Carroll as the heroine of Alice in Wonderland, stayed at the St Tudno at the age of eight on her first visit to Llandudno in 1861.

In good weather, take tea on the patio and enjoy outstanding views over the bay. In winter, choose one of three beautifully designed lounges. The menu offers two set teas – the Full Afternoon Tea with sandwiches, scones, Bara Brith, Welsh Cakes and home-made cakes, and the De-Luxe Afternoon Tea which includes the full afternoon tea and adds smoked salmon sandwiches, strawberries and cream and a glass of champagne. *Teas served:* Assam, Darjeeling, Ceylon, Lapsang Souchong, Earl Grey, 2 House Blends – Yorkshire Gold Medal and English Breakfast, decaffeinated and a fine selection of loose leaf teas are available. *Fruit flavoured teas and herbal infusions are also offered.*

GWALIA TEA ROOMS

Owner: Mike Morton

**The Museum of Welsh Life
St Fagans, Cardiff
CF5 6XB
Tel: 01222 566985
Fax: 01222 566985**

Directions
Take exit 33 off the M4 and follow signs to

The Museum of Welsh Life. The tearooms are within the grounds of the museum.

Opening times
**Open all year except Christmas Day,
Boxing Day and New Year's Day,
10 am–4.45 pm.**

Local Interest:
The tea shop is within the grounds of the Museum of Welsh Life which has a complete Welsh village with blacksmith, school, old cottages, an old photographer's shop and lots more.

Gwalia Tea Rooms are situated on the first floor of Gwalia Stores, a high class department store that was moved stone by stone from the coal-mining village of Ogmore Vale and meticulously rebuilt within the grounds of The Museum of Welsh Life. The interior, once the corn store, is decorated and furnished in the authentic style of the 1920s, with bentwood chairs, old mirrors, a cut glass screen at one end of the room and old photos of the building in its original setting. To get to the tearoom, you have to pass through the old-fashioned ironmongery downstairs where you can still buy an old tin bath, if you want to. However, you might be more interested in the jams and pickles and other home-made goodies.

The tea-time menu is as traditional as the shop surroundings and includes, of course, Welsh cakes and Bara Brith, which Mike Morton sends out mail order to people who tried it once and now want more. And custard slices are a regular treat, again following a tradition from the days when Mr Llewellyn, who ran Gwalia Stores back in Ogmore Vale, baked them every Friday. *Teas served:* Darjeeling, Assam, Ceylon, Earl Grey, Lapsang Souchong, Jasmine, Gunpowder, Oolong, Yunnan, Rose Pouchong. *Fruit flavoured teas and herbal infusions are also available.*

CELTIC FARE TEAROOMS

Owner: Mr and Mrs C. Phillips

Vernon House, St Julians Street
Tenby, Pembrokeshire SA70 7AS
Tel: 01834 845258

Directions

Take the A478 into Tenby and the Celtic Fare Tearooms is half way down St Julians Street on the left hand side, very close to the Harbour and Castle Beach.

Opening times
Open all year.
Monday–Sunday, 10 am–5.30 pm.

Awards
1993   Tea Council Award of Excellence

Local Interest:
You can walk around the old town walls and visit the 14th century Tudor merchant's house (now run by The National Trust), the museum, lifeboat station and aquarium. Fishing trips go from the harbour and boat trips leave every half hour to Caldey Island which is 20 minutes away and has a Cistercian monastery.

Celtic Fare is a real traditional Welsh tearoom serving home-baked cakes, pastries and savouries of a very high standard. In its first year it won a Tea Council Award of Excellence and deserves to be packed all the time with appreciative, hungry customers.

The attraction starts right at the front door to this eye-catching building where bright hanging baskets surround the pretty door and windows. Inside, there is a feeling of warmth and welcome. The old beams are hung with jugs and teapots, lamps cast a warm glow over the cosy, friendly room and there is a real fire in the Victorian hearth and fresh flowers around the room. The Celtic spirit is heightened by the soothing traditional music playing in the background and the really tempting freshly baked Welsh cakes, hot from the griddle and scones served with lashings of Caldey Island clotted cream and fruity jam.

Light snacks are available all day and you can lunch on Welsh rarebits or Heggarty Pie with crisp bacon topping, or take tea with tangy lemon torte, apple cake and fresh fruit pavlovas. The display on the counter will make it really difficult for you to choose. *Teas served:* House Blend, Earl Grey, Darjeeling, Ceylon, Lapsang Souchong. *Fruit flavoured teas and herbal infusions are also offered.*

THE OLD STATION COFFEE SHOP

Owner: Eileen Minter

Dinas Mawddwy
Machynlleth
Powys SY20 9LS
Tel: 01650 531338

Directions
The A470 (the main North to South Wales road) passes the gate to Meirion Mill by Minllyn Bridge one mile north of the A470 junction with the A458 at Mallwyd. The Old Station Coffee Shop is on the right, inside the gate to the Mill.

Opening times
Open March–mid-November.
Monday–Sunday, 9.30 am–5 pm.

Awards
Egon Ronay recommended

Local Interest:
Meirion Mill is in what were the old slate engine sheds. The working looms produce cloth and garments that are for sale in the Mill shop. There are walks and climbs in all directions.

The Old Station stands beneath high conifers at the side of a disused railway line in an area of Wales steeped in legend and history and where King Arthur is said to have fought his last battle. Visitors may walk for miles to explore the surrounding Dinas Mawddwy mountains and countryside that create the backdrop for the old station building. The original waiting room is now two tearooms that still have the old-fashioned station fireplaces and are furnished with pine chairs, tables and dressers. Outside, on the old platform, there are slate tables, teak benches, fresh flowers and plants in tubs and cascading baskets, and an old station sign to remind you of the days when steam engines pulled their heavy load of freight and passengers through the breathtaking Welsh scenery.

Eileen's menu is deliciously Welsh, and the cheese scones, the Bara Brith and other cakes are so good that people travel hundreds of miles to taste them. The lunchtime menu offers home-made soups, pizzas, quiches, salads, sandwiches and four different ploughmans. Welsh cakes, other whole cakes, honeys, preserves and ice creams are on sale to take away. *Teas served:* Indian, Darjeeling, Assam, English Breakfast, Earl Grey, Lady Grey, China, decaffeinated. *Herbal infusions are also available.*

S C O T L A N D
R E G I O N A L   M A P

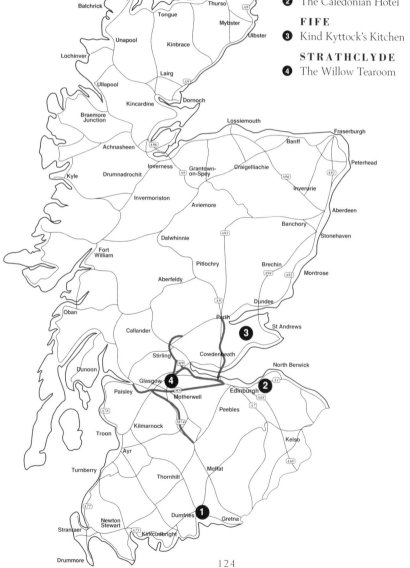

ABBEY COTTAGE TEA ROOMS

Owners: Morag McKie and
Jacqui Wilson

**26 Main Street, New Abbey
Dumfries DG2 8BY
Tel: 01387 850377**

Directions
Take the A710 from Dumfries to New Abbey
(the Solway Coast Road). Abbey Cottage is
beside Sweetheart Abbey. The Village Car Park
is behind.

Opening times
Open 1st April–31st October and
weekends to Christmas.
Monday–Sunday, 10 am–5.30 pm.

Awards
Egon Ronay recommended

Local Interest:
*Wander around the Abbey ruins and learn the story of
Lady Devorgilla. Also visit the Shambellie House Museum of
Costume and an 18th century water mill that still operates.*

If you take the Solway Coast Road from Dumfries, you will drive through some wonderful countryside before you find yourself in the quiet village of New Abbey. Here stand the rose-coloured remains of Sweetheart Abbey, built by Lady Devorgilla in the 13th century in memory of her husband, John Balliol, with whom she founded Balliol College, Oxford.

Just across the road from the medieval ruins, 19th century Abbey Cottage offers a warm welcome and a delicious selection of healthy home-made specialities that are served in a friendly, caring, non-smoking environment. Morag McKie and her daughter Jacqui use high-quality local produce and include low-fat and vegetarian options on their menu. Home-made soups, granary breads, Scottish country pâté and tasty sandwiches or salads are perfect for a light lunch, while the tea-time selection includes Jacqui's excellent carrot or banana cake, and plain, wholemeal or fruit scones that are served with Morag's home-made jams. In good weather, enjoy your tea in the garden at the back of the pretty cottage and before leaving, visit the craft shop next door to browse amongst the very attractive range of local pottery, candles and table wares. *Teas served*: Traditional Blend, Assam, Darjeeling, Earl Grey and decaffeinated. *Fruit flavoured teas and herbal infusions are also offered.*

THE CALEDONIAN HOTEL

General Manager: Stephen Carter

Princes Street
Edinburgh EH1 2AB
Tel: 0131 459 9988 Fax: 0131 225 6632

Directions
The Caledonian is situated at the west end of Princes Street, adjoining Lothian Road.

Opening times
Open all year.
Afternoon tea is served from 3–5.30 pm.

Awards
1996 Tea Council Award of Excellence

Local Interest:
Within walking distance lie Edinburgh Castle and other historic buildings, and Princes Street's main shops.

The "Caley" (the locals' affectionate name for the Caledonian Hotel) occupies a prominent position in one of Scotland's finest streets. The view of Edinburgh Castle from the windows of the lounge is spectacular and the setting creates an interesting and relaxing location for informal lunches and gracious afternoon teas between shopping and sightseeing. The menu offers a sparkling selection of wonderful sandwiches with truly imaginative fillings and toppings – mozzarella, plum tomatoes and pesto, Angus minute steak with mustard and onions, chicken mayonnaise with Swiss cheese and crispy bacon. And the traditional Afternoon Tea consists of finger sandwiches, scones and home-made cakes such as Dundee, cherry and Madeira cake. For a special occasion, choose the Celebration Tea with its added glass of Champagne, or simply enjoy a pot of tea and a traditional Scotch pancake. *Teas served:* Breakfast Blend, Assam, Ceylon, Darjeeling, Earl Grey, Lapsang Souchong, Keemun. *Fruit flavoured teas and herbal infusions are also available.*

KIND KYTTOCK'S KITCHEN

Owners: Liz and Bert Dalrymple

**Cross Wynd, Falkland
Fife, KY15 7BE
Tel: 01337 857477**

Directions

Follow signs from the M90 for Falkland Palace. Cross Wynd joins the High Street at the fountain and Mercat Cross.

Opening times
**Open all year except Mondays and two weeks from Christmas Day–January 5th.
Tuesday–Sunday, 10.30 am–5.30 pm.**

Awards
1991 & 92   Tea Council Award of Excellence
Egon Ronay recommended

Local Interest:
Falkland Palace, at the centre of the village, was built by James IV in the 16th century. The gardens and tennis court – one of the oldest in Britain – are well worth a visit.

Kind Kyttock was the heroine of a poem by William Dunbar, the early Scots poet. 'The Ballad of Kind Kyttock' tells how she settled in Falkland and served good food and drink to weary travellers. Liz and Bert Dalrymple, who came here from Glasgow 25 years ago to find a more peaceful life, follow her example and offer tasty traditional Scottish fare in a relaxed atmosphere to thousands of visitors every year from all over the world. In fact, a group of Americans arrived one day with a cutting from the *Los Angeles Times* giving a very positive review of Kind Kyttock's, so news of how good it is has obviously spread far and wide.

The menu has an appealing Scottish flavour – Midlothian oatcakes served with cheddar cheese, Scottish pancakes with cream and home-made apricot jam or fresh fruit, traditional Cloutie Dumpling with cream, and an irresistible Rob Roy ice cream with butterscotch sauce and petticoat tail shortbread. All these good things are served in two rooms, upstairs and down, where dark furniture, colourful tablecloths and an interesting selection of prints and paintings on the walls create a very pleasing, old-fashioned atmosphere. *Teas served:* House Blend, Darjeeling, Earl Grey, China, Ceylon, Assam, Russian. *Herbal infusions are also offered.*

THE WILLOW TEAROOM

Owner: Anne Mulhern

217 Sauchiehall Street
Glasgow G2 3EX
Tel: 0141 332 0521

Directions
The tearoom is on the first floor above
Henderson the jewellers.

Opening times
Open all year.
Monday–Saturday, 9.30 am–4.30 pm.
Sunday, 12 noon–4 pm.

Awards
Egon Ronay recommended

Local Interest:
Within walking distance of the tearoom is the Glasgow
School of Art, the Tenement House (a reconstruction of a
typical Glaswegian tenement block with original domestic
interiors), the Glasgow Concert Hall and the Kelvin Grove
Museum. There are also many other examples of
Mackintosh architecture.

While tea shops often manage to create an impression of past times, the Willow Tearoom is a genuine example of turn-of-the-century design. The Room de Luxe is the only remaining room of Miss Kate Cranston's 'tearoom empire', created for her by Charles Rennie Mackintosh in 1904. His wonderful Arts and Crafts style that heralded Art Deco, gave his architecture, furniture, lamps and tableware the strong rectilinear contours and geometric shapes that fascinate the eye. Mackintosh had previously designed the interior for three other Cranston tearooms, but the Willow allowed him to style the exterior and interior of an entire building.

In 1983, the tearoom was restored by the current owner, Anne Mulhern. The mirror friezes, the gesso panel and the ornate leaded doors had happily survived and the chairs and tables were reproduced to Mackintosh's original 1904 design. An unhurried atmosphere matches the elegance of the interior and the comprehensive list of teas, favourite tea-time traditionals and cakes makes this a very special experience. *Teas served:* Tearoom Blend, Breakfast, Earl Grey, Lapsang Souchong, Darjeeling, Ceylon, Assam, Rose Petal, Keemun, Jasmine Blossom, Yunnan, Kenya, Rose Pouchong, decaffeinated. *Fruit flavoured teas and herbal infusions are also offered.*

LOCATION OF GUILD TEA SHOPS

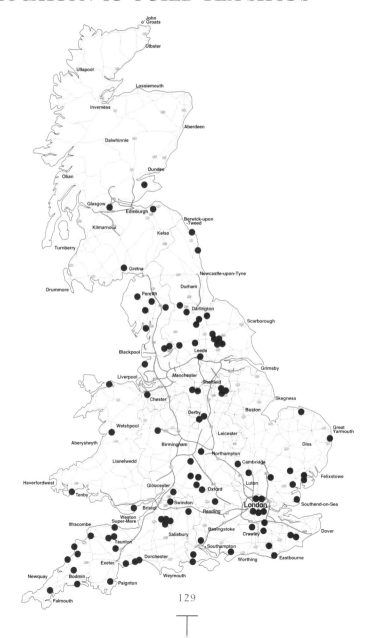

129

INDEX OF TEA SHOPS

ENGLAND

WALES

SCOTLAND

LEADING UK TEA SUPPLIERS

UK Blenders & Packers
Accord Services Ltd
Ahmad Tea Ltd
Barber Kingsmark Ltd
Big T (Tea) Ltd
   Ismail & Co Ltd
Brodie Melrose Drysdale & Co Ltd
Burnham Trading Co Ltd
Char Wallahs Ltd
Chelsea Foods Ltd
Cooper & Co
D J Miles & Co
Gala Coffee & Tea Ltd
George Payne & Co Ltd
George Williamson & Co Ltd
Hankow Batchelor Tea Co Ltd
Imporient (UK) Ltd
Kamet Ltd
Keith Spicer & Co Ltd
Langdons (Coffee & Tea) Ltd
London & Scottish International Ltd
Matthew Algie & Co Ltd

Nairobi Coffee & Tea Co Ltd
Netherbourne Foods Ltd
New English Teas Ltd
Norfolk Tea & Coffee Co
Northern Tea Merchants
Premier Beverages
   Glengettie Tea Co Ltd
   London Herb & Spice Co Ltd
   Melroses Ltd
   Ridgways
Ringtons Ltd
R Twining & Co Ltd
   Jacksons of Piccadilly Ltd
   Namosa Ltd
Taylors of Harrogate
Tetley GB Ltd
Tudor Tea & Coffee
Unilever Export International
Van den Bergh Foods Ltd
Whittard of Chelsea Ltd
Windmill Tea & Coffee Ltd

A member of The Tea Council

The Tea Council

Guild of Tea Shops